God's BIG Story

Reading | Level 1

By R. A. Sheats
Illustrations by Edmilson Cotrim dos Santos Cotrim

Generations
PASSING ON THE FAITH

ISBN: 978-1-954745-00-1

Cover Design: Justin Turley
Cover Illustration: Matthew Sample II
Interior Layout Design: Sarah Lee Bryant

Published by:
Generations
19039 Plaza Drive Ste 210
Parker, Colorado 80134
www.generations.org

For more information on this and
other titles from Generations,
visit www.generations.org or call 888-389-9080.

CONTENTS

TO THE PARENT
AND TEACHER

Welcome to *God's Big Story*! It is our joy to partner with you in the glorious task of introducing young minds to the eternal truths contained in the Word of our gracious and loving God.

This coursework is intended to serve as an aid to parents who are looking for a Christian Family Discipleship approach to the education of their children. Christian education is always parent integrated, Bible integrated, and life integrated. This is the clear philosophy of education visible in Deuteronomy 6:6-9, Ephesians 6:4, and the book of Proverbs. *God's Big Story* seeks to follow this biblical mandate by introducing children to Scripture and to the faith and life lessons to be gleaned from it. This curriculum focuses on nurturing children in the faith, in Christ, and in Christian character. Every chapter of this reading course will familiarize students with a new historical passage from Scripture and will teach the child how to learn from and apply the truths contained in each biblical account.

Best Book Approach

Nowadays it's fashionable to introduce "great books" to our children in their Christian paideia or educational training. We, however, recommend the best Book—the Bible. If our children want to learn to read and think, the first and core content of their study must be the Bible. These are God's stories, and our children should know all the stories of Scripture by the time they are reading on a fifth grade level.

Avoiding the piecemeal approach to Bible stories, the authors of this course instead present the whole story, the unity of Scripture, the true message intended by God. It is a redemptive story. While there may be moral lessons to glean here and there, the core message of Scripture is the work of God in redemption. This is the story the Bible presents from cover to cover and is the story focused on in this reading course. If our children learn a thousand other stories but miss this one, we have neglected our duty in their education.

The key objectives of this program are:

1. To provide the child with a clear understanding of biblical vocabulary to prepare them to read a substantive English translation of the Bible on their own.
2. To grant the child a familiarity with the full scope of biblical stories, the historical narrative of God's revelation.

3. To master the entire theme of the Bible, the Christ-focus of Scripture, and the fulfillment of the Old Testament in the New Testament.
4. To believe the Gospel.
5. To worship God, to fear God, and to obey His Word.

Our authors have been careful to present the wide range of scriptural stories without censorship. However, care has been taken to present stories on a level of understanding appropriate for six-year-olds.

Scriptural quotations at the end of each chapter are taken from the New King James Version of the Bible. This version has also been used where narratives and conversations in the text include word-for-word scriptural quotations.

God's Big Story Level 1 has been designed to be used as a reading book during the second semester of first grade, after the child has already begun a basic phonics curriculum and has learned the elementary principles of pronunciation. This book is intended to be used in conjunction with the selection of read-aloud books that form a part of the Generations first grade reading curriculum.

May the Spirit of our God anoint these readings and studies to the spiritual enlightenment, the spiritual life, and the spiritual growth of the students.

Generations Curriculum Team

January 2021

CHAPTER 1

God Makes a Good World

God made all things. He has a plan. It is a good plan.

God said, "I will make light." God makes the light. The light is good. God makes all things good. This is Day One.

On Day Two, God makes the sky. God sees the sky. It is good.

On Day Three, God makes the sea. He makes the dry land. He said, "Let grass grow on the land. Let trees and plants grow." The land obeys God. The

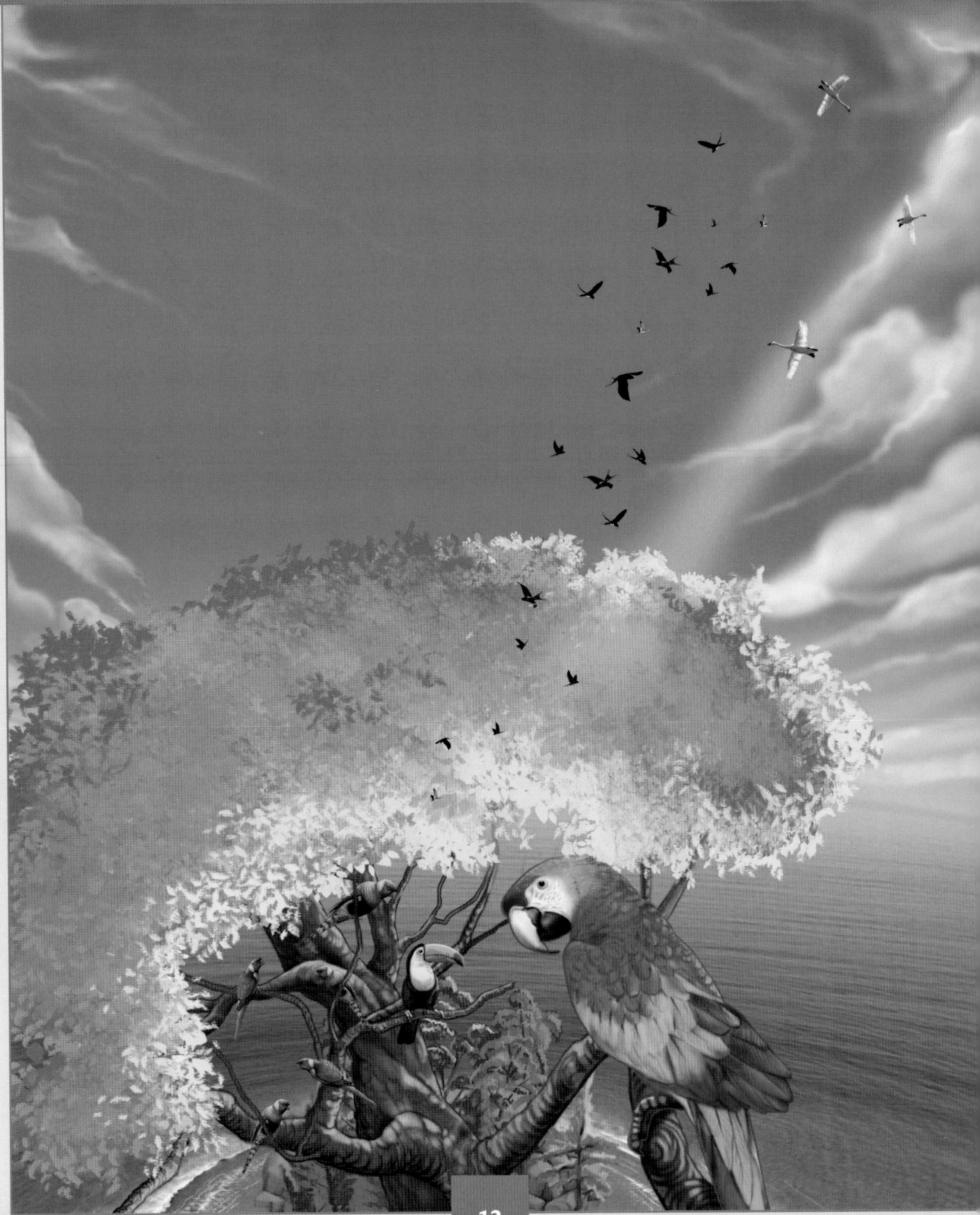

grass **grows**. The trees and plants **grow**. God sees His work. It is **good**. stop M

On Day Four, God makes the sun and the moon. He makes the stars, too. The sun shines on the land. It shines on the grass and the trees. God sees the sun and moon and stars. His work is **good**. Will God make man yet? No, not yet.

On Day Five, God makes the fish. He makes the birds. God will bless the fish and the birds. He will tell them to **grow** and fill the land and sea. Will the fish and birds **obey** God? Yes, they will **obey**. God sees His work. It is **good**.

On Day Six, God makes the **creatures** that live on the land. He makes pigs. He makes dogs. He makes bugs. He makes all **creatures** on the land. God sees that this is **good**.

Next, God said, "Let Us make man in Our **image**. Let them rule the fish and the birds and all things.

Let them rule the land I made." God makes man. He makes Adam and Eve. He will bless them. He tells Adam and Eve, "Fill the land. Rule the fish and the birds and the cows. Rule all the creatures." Will man obey God?

God sees His world. He sees all He made. It is good.

On Day Seven, God will rest. He has made the land. He has made the sea. He has made the fish and the birds. He has made the cows and the bugs. He has made man. He will end His work. God will bless this day. He will rest on this day, and we will rest, too.

God makes His world. His world is good.

> Then God said, "Let there be light";
> and there was light. (Genesis 1:3) stop T.

W

Faith Lessons

God has a plan — God makes all things. He has a plan for the world. He has a plan for man.

God is a wise and good God — God made the world. He is a wise God. He is good. He sees all things and makes them good.

God rests on Day Seven — God rests on this day. We will rest on this day, too. God makes a day for His world to rest.

Vocabulary

light	creature	world
good	image	wise
obey	Adam	

CHAPTER 2

Adam and Eve Sin

God made a **garden**. He will give Adam a **law**. The **law** is good. God tells Adam, "Rule the **garden**. Rule the plants and the bugs and all things." Adam must obey God. Will Adam obey?

God will give Adam a **helper**. He will make Eve. Eve will help Adam. Adam and Eve will work in the **garden**. They will rule the plants. They will rule the birds and the fish.

God will give Adam a **law**. God will give a good **law**. He says, "Eat the **fruit** in the **garden**. But do not

eat the fruit of this tree." Adam and Eve must not eat from this tree. Will Adam and Eve obey God?

The devil sees Adam and Eve. The devil is bad. He will not obey God. He tells Eve, "God is not good. He tells you bad things. Will you eat the fruit? The fruit is good. Do not obey God."

Eve sees the **devil**. She sees the **fruit**. Will she obey the **devil**? Yes, she will obey. She will not obey God.

Adam sees the **fruit**. He will eat the **fruit**. He will not obey God. Adam will sin. Eve will sin.

God sees Adam and Eve. He will ask, "Did you eat the **fruit**?"

Adam is sad. Eve is sad. Sin will make them sad. Sin will kill them. Can God fix this?

God will tell Adam, "You did not obey. You did sin. But I will **save** you from sin. I will send a Seed. He will stop the **devil**. The Seed will crush him. The Seed will **save** you."

God sees His world. He sees the bad in His world. But God will make His world good. He will **save** Adam from sin. He will **save** Eve from sin. God is **strong**. God is wise. He is good. He can **save** us from sin.

Then the LORD God called to Adam and said to him, "Where are you?" (Genesis 3:9)

Faith Lessons

Adam did not obey — God is good. He gives a good law. We must trust Him. We must obey His law.

Sin kills — We sin if we do not obey God and His law. Sin is bad. It will kill you. We must run from sin. We must run to God.

God can save from sin — We sin like Adam. I am bad. You are bad. We all sin. But God can save us from sin. He sent a Seed. The Seed is Jesus Christ.

Vocabulary

garden	fruit	strong
law	devil	
helper	save	

CHAPTER 3

God Sends a Flood

God made all things. He made plants. He made fish. He made bugs. He made all things good. God sees His world. It is good.

Adam sins. Eve sins. They do not obey God. They do bad things.

God sees His world. It is not good. God sees sin.

God sees dads and moms. Dads and moms sin.

God sees boys and girls. Boys and girls sin. Do you sin?

God said, "I am sad that I made man. I will **destroy**

him. I will **destroy** the birds and the bugs and the pigs. I will **destroy** them, for man did sin."

Will God **destroy** all men? No, He will not. God made a **promise**. He said He will send a Seed. The Seed will save **people** from sin. God will keep His **promise**.

God sees Noah. Noah is a good man. Will Noah sin? Yes, he will sin. But Noah will **fear** God.

God tells Noah, "I will **destroy** all things. I will send a **flood**. The **flood** will kill all men and all things. But I will save you. Make an **ark**. The **ark** will keep you safe."

Noah will trust God. He will make the **ark**. His sons will help.

God will send birds to Noah. He will

send bugs. He will send cats and pigs. Noah will put them in the ark. He will get food for them. He will obey God.

Noah tells people not to sin. He says, "Obey God." But the people do not obey. They will sin. They do not love God.

God will send rain. He will send a flood. The flood will kill all things. All men will die. Why will they die? God hates sin.

God will keep Noah safe. He will keep his sons safe. He will keep them safe in the ark.

God will end the flood. He will stop the rain. He will stop the flood.

He will tell Noah, "Come out of the ark."

Noah will come out. He sees the land. He sees the mud. He will fear God. He will love God.

God sees Noah. God said, "I will keep you safe. I will make a promise. I will not send a flood again."

God will make a **rain-bow**. The **rainbow** is His **promise**. Noah sees the **rainbow**. He is glad.

God will love Noah. God will keep His **promise**. God is good.

But Noah found grace in the eyes of the L*ORD*.

(Genesis 6:8)

Faith Lessons

God hates sin — Sin is bad. God hates sin. Do you hate sin?

God will punish sin — Did God punish the world? Yes, He did. He sent a flood. One day He will punish all the world for sin. One day Jesus will come and punish the world for sin.

Noah will fear God — Noah will sin. But he will fear God. He will be sad for his sin. He will trust God. God will save him. Can you trust God?

God makes a promise — God will promise to save Noah from the flood. He will keep His promise. He loves Noah. He loves His world. He is a good God. He will keep His promise.

Vocabulary

destroy	fear	people
promise	flood	rainbow
Noah	ark	

CHAPTER 4

The Tower of Babel

Noah will come out of the ark. His sons will come out. Noah and his sons will live in the land. They will live in the land God made.

Noah has sons. His sons have sons. Soon lots of boys and girls live in the land. Lots of moms and dads live in the land. Will the people be good? Will they obey God?

God said to Noah and his sons, "Fill the land. Have lots of kids. Live in the land I made. Fill the land I give you."

Noah had sons. His sons had sons. They had lots and lots of kids. Will they fill the land? Will they obey God?

The people will not obey God. They will not fill the land. They will live in one land. They will not fear God.

The people said, "We will make a city. We will make a tower. We will make the city big. We will make the tower tall. We will be safe here. We will have one city. We will have one tower. We will be one."

The people will name the city Babel.

Will the city make the people safe? Will the tower make the people safe? Will it make the people strong?

The people do not trust God. They do not fear God.

God sees the city. He sees the tower. He said, "The people are bad. They trust in a city. They trust in a tower. This is not good. They do not trust in Me."

Then God said, "I will stop the people. They will not make the city. They will not make the tower. I will scatter them. They will not be one."

Did God scatter the people? Yes, He did. He sent the people away. They did not live in the city. They did not live in the **tower**. They left the **city**. They did **scatter** in the land.

Now the people will fill the land. Will the people do what God said?

So the L*ORD* *scattered them.*

(Genesis 11:8)

Faith Lessons

God will stop bad people — The people did not obey God. They did not trust God. They did not fill the land. God said, "I will scatter the people." God will not help the city. He will stop the people. They will scatter. God is strong. He will stop bad people.

God will keep His promise — Did the people sin? Yes, they did sin. But God will keep His promise. He will not kill all the people. He will send a Seed. He will send Someone to save the people from sin.

Vocabulary

city	safe	help
tower	Babel	
tall	scatter	

CHAPTER 5

God's Promise to Abraham

God will **call** a man. The man is **A-bra-ham**. God tells him, "I will bless you. Obey Me and **walk** with Me."

Abraham will trust God. He will obey God. He will fear God.

Abraham has a wife. Her name is **Sarah**. **Sarah** has no **baby**. **Sarah** is sad. **Abraham** is sad.

God said to **Abraham**, "I will bless you. I will give you a son." Will **Abraham** trust God? Will **Sarah** trust God?

Sarah said, "I am old. Will God give me a son?"

Abraham is sad. He said, "God, I have no son. Will You give me a son?"

But God said to him, "Look up at the stars. Can you count them?"

Abraham will look at the stars. He can not count

them.

God said, "Your sons will be like the stars. You can not **count** the stars. You can not **count** your sons. I will bless you. I will give you a land. I will give your sons a land."

Then God said, "I will bless you. I will bless all people in you. I will bless all people in your seed."

God will make a promise with **Abraham**. Will God keep His promise? Yes, He will keep it.

Abraham will trust God. **Sarah** will trust God. **Sarah** will have a son. She will name him **Isaac**.

Now **Abraham** is glad. Now **Sarah** is glad. They have a son. They have **Isaac**.

God is good. He gives **Abraham** a son. He makes a promise. And He keeps His promise. God is very good.

And Abraham called the name of his son . . . Isaac.

(Genesis 21:3)

Faith Lessons

God calls Abraham — God will call Abraham. He will tell him to obey. He will tell him to trust God. He will bless Abraham.

God will bless all people in Abraham — God will send a son to Abraham. One day He will send a Seed. This Seed will come through Abraham's son. The Seed is Jesus Christ. God will bless all people in this Seed. He will bless all people in Jesus Christ.

Abraham will trust God — Abraham has no son. He is sad. But he will trust God. God will keep His promise. Will you trust God?

Vocabulary

call	Sarah	Isaac
Abraham	baby	
walk	count	

CHAPTER 6

Isaac Finds a Wife

Abraham has a son. His son is Isaac. Abraham is glad to have a son. He will **teach** his son. He will **teach** Isaac.

Abraham will **teach** Isaac to love God. He will **teach** him to fear God. He will **teach** him to obey.

Isaac will **grow** up. He will be a man.

Abraham sees his son. His son is a man. Abraham says, "My son will need a wife." Can Abraham **find** a wife for Isaac?

Abraham will call a man. Abraham will trust this

man. He will tell the man, "I need a wife for my son. This wife must love God. She must fear God. She must trust God. You must look for her. You must find a wife for Isaac."

The man will obey. He will ride a camel. He will go far away. He will look for a wife for Isaac. Will he find a wife?

The man will pray to God. He will say, "God, You are strong. You are wise. You will be good to Abraham. Please send a wife for Isaac."

The man will stop at a well. His camel will want water.

Soon a woman will come to the well. Her name is Re-be-kah. The man sees Rebekah. Will she be a wife for Isaac?

Rebekah sees the man. She sees the camel. She tells the man, "I will give your camel water."

Rebekah is a good woman. She loves God. She

trusts God. She fears God.

The man sees Rebekah. He will ask her to be a wife for Isaac.

Did God hear the man pray? Yes, He did hear. He

sent **Rebekah** to be a wife for Isaac. God is kind to the man. He is kind to Abraham. He is kind to Isaac.

The man brings **Rebekah** home. Isaac sees **Rebekah**. He will love her. He will take her as his wife.

Now Abraham is glad. Now Isaac is glad. Now **Rebekah** is glad. God is good.

> *He took Rebekah and she became his wife,*
> *and he loved her.*
> *(Genesis 24:67)*

Faith Lessons

God loves His people — God was kind to Abraham. He loves Abraham. He is a good God. He is a kind God.

God hears us pray — Did the man pray to God? Yes, he did. Did God hear the man pray? Yes, He did hear. He will hear us pray, too. We must trust God just like Abraham.

God is strong and wise — Isaac needs a wife. He can not find her. But God can find her. God is strong. He is wise. We must trust Him.

Vocabulary

teach	camel	woman
grow	pray	Rebekah
find	water	

CHAPTER 7

God Blesses Jacob

Isaac has a wife. Her name is Rebekah. Isaac and Rebekah are sad. They have no son. What will they do?

Isaac will pray. He will trust God. Will God hear Isaac pray? Yes, God will hear. God is good. He will give Isaac a son.

Rebekah has a son. Will she have one son? No, she will have two sons. God will give her two sons. They will be twins. The sons are Jacob and Esau.

Isaac will teach his sons. But will his sons obey? No,

his sons will sin.

God sees Isaac. He sees Jacob and Esau. God sees all people sin. God hates sin. But He will have mercy on His people. God will be kind. He will love Isaac.

He will love Jacob. God will have mercy.

Esau is a strong man. He will hunt. He will be strong. But he will not obey God. He will find a wife. His wife will not trust God. His wife will not love God.

Jacob is not nice to Esau. Esau is not nice to Jacob.

God sees Jacob. He will have mercy on Jacob. Jacob is bad, but God will be kind. He will love Jacob. He will teach Jacob to fear God. He will teach Jacob to obey.

Isaac will call Jacob. He will tell him, "Go find a wife. Find a wife who will fear God. Find a wife who will love God."

Isaac tells Jacob, "God will bless you. God made a promise to Abraham. He will keep His promise. He will keep you safe. He will give you a wife. He will give you a land."

Jacob went far away. He went to look for a wife.

The road was long. Jacob got tired. He went to sleep.

God came to Jacob. God said, "I am the God of Abraham. I am the God of Isaac. I will be your God. I will bless you."

God tells Jacob, "I will give you a wife. I will give you sons. I will give you a land. I will be with you. I will keep you safe."

Jacob is glad. He will trust God. Will God keep him safe? Yes, God will keep him safe.

Jacob will find a wife. Jacob will have sons. God will give him 12 sons. God will bless Jacob. God will have mercy on him.

"Behold, I am with you and will keep you wherever you go, and will bring you back to this land."
(Genesis 28:15)

Faith Lessons

Isaac prays — Isaac was sad. Rebekah was sad. They did not have a son. But Isaac prays to God. God will hear him pray. God will give him a son.

God has mercy — Isaac sins. Jacob sins. But God will have mercy on them. Jacob is bad. But God will be kind. He will teach Jacob to love God. He will teach Jacob to fear God.

Vocabulary

twins	people	away
Jacob	mercy	tired
Esau	nice	

CHAPTER 8

Joseph and His Brothers

Jacob had 12 sons. He **loved** his sons. But he **loved** his son **Joseph** best.

Jacob gave **Joseph** a gift. The gift was a coat. The coat had lots of **colors** on it.

Joseph was glad to have the coat. But his **brothers** were not glad. They were mad. They did not like **Joseph**. They did not like his coat. They **hated Joseph**.

Joseph went to sleep. He had a dream. In his dream, he saw 11 stars. The stars were his **brothers**. The stars **bowed** down to him.

He saw the sun in his dream. The sun **bowed** down to him. He saw the moon. The moon **bowed** down to him.

Joseph told his **brothers** the dream. His **brothers**

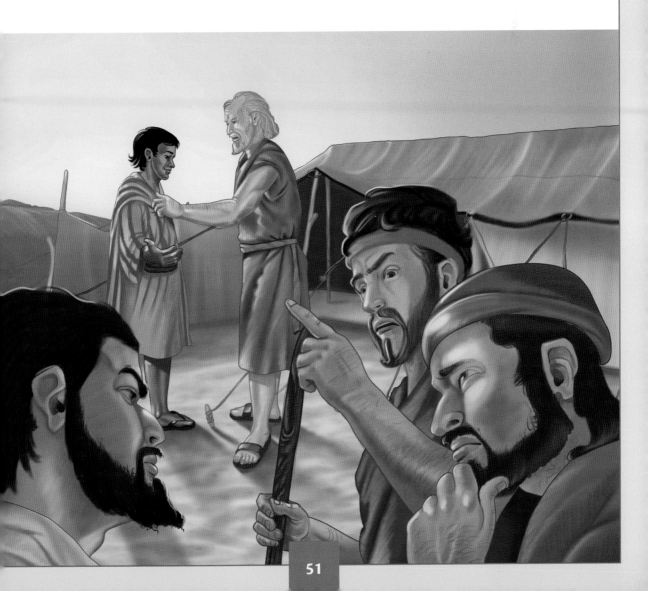

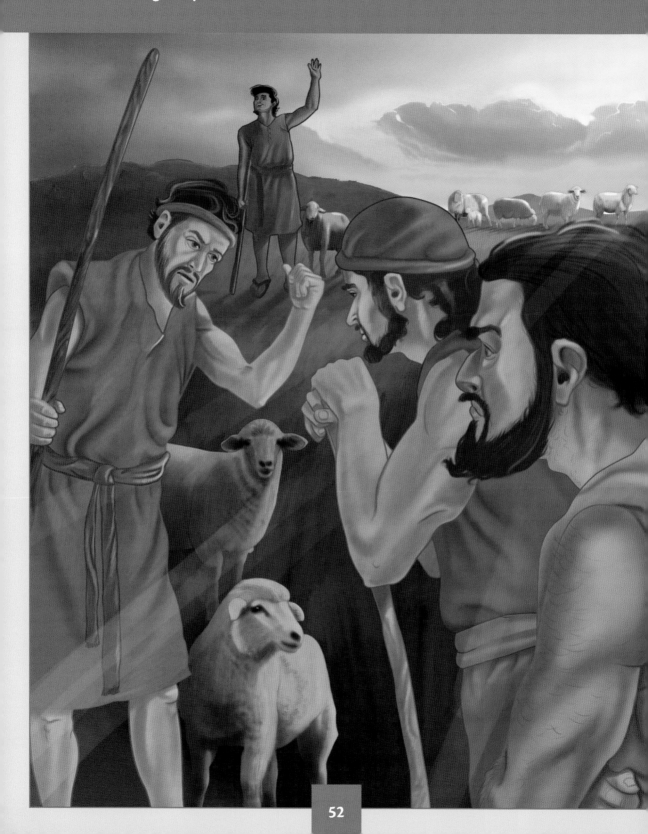

were mad. "We will not bow down to you!" they said. They hated his dream. They hated Joseph.

One day, the brothers went out with the goats and sheep. They went to keep the goats and sheep safe.

Jacob said to Joseph, "Go find your brothers." Will Joseph obey? Yes, he will obey. Joseph trusts God. He loves God. He will obey Jacob.

Joseph went out to the goats. His brothers saw him. They were mad. They hated Joseph. They took his coat. They put him in a pit.

"We will kill him!" they said. But the brothers did not kill Joseph. They took him out of the pit. "We will sell him as a slave," they said.

Joseph did not want to be a slave. "Please do not do this!" he said.

But his brothers were mad. They sold Joseph as a slave.

Joseph was very sad.

Joseph had a coat. The brothers took the coat. They put blood on the coat. They gave it to Jacob.

Jacob saw the coat. "Joseph is dead. My son is dead," he said. Jacob was sad.

Now Joseph is a slave. He is sad. He prays to God. Will God hear him?

Did God see the brothers? Did God see them sin? Will He help Joseph?

Joseph is very sad. He will pray to God. He will trust in God.

Now Joseph had a dream, and he told it to his brothers; and they hated him even more.
(Genesis 37:5)

Faith Lessons

The brothers hated Joseph — The brothers did not love Joseph. They hated him. This is sin. The brothers were not good. They did not love God.

Joseph will trust in God — Joseph is very sad. He is a slave. But he will trust God. He will pray to God.

God sees all things — God saw the brothers sin. He saw Joseph in the pit. He saw what the brothers did. He sees you. He sees me. God sees all things.

Vocabulary

loved	brothers	sold
Joseph	hated	blood
colors	bowed	dead

CHAPTER 9

Joseph is a Slave

Joseph was a slave. Bad men took him to Egypt. They sold him to a man. Now Joseph was a slave to the man in Egypt.

Joseph was sad. He did not like to be in Egypt. He did not like to be a slave. But he trusted in God. Did God see him? Yes, God saw him. Joseph said, "I will trust God. He is good."

Joseph served the man in Egypt. Joseph obeyed the man. He did not want to be a slave. But he did what was good. He obeyed the man.

God saw Joseph. He saw Joseph in Egypt. He said, "I will bless Joseph."

The man saw Joseph. He saw Joseph was good. He said, "Joseph is a good man. I will trust him." The

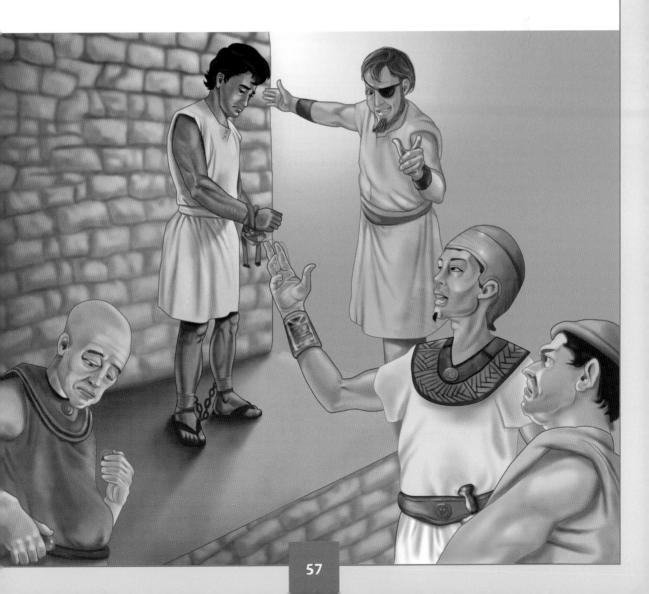

man said, "I will let Joseph keep my home safe."

Joseph did good things. He kept the man's home safe.

The man in **Egypt** had a wife. The wife saw Joseph. She **wanted** Joseph to be bad. She said, "Come sin with me."

Joseph did not want to sin. He did not want to be with the man's wife. He **wanted** to obey God. He said, "I can not sin. I must obey God."

The wife got mad. She hated Joseph. She **wanted** to sin, but Joseph did not want to sin.

The man came home. His wife told a lie. She said, "Joseph is bad. He wants to sin. You can not trust him."

The man **heard** his wife. He got mad at Joseph. "You are bad!" he said. He put Joseph in **prison**.

Joseph was very sad. He did not want the wife to lie. He did not want the man to get mad. He did not

want to be in prison.

Joseph said, "I did not sin. Why am I in prison?"

Joseph was very sad. But he trusted God. "God sees me," he said. "God is good. I will trust Him."

God saw the man in Egypt. God saw the man's wife. God heard the wife lie.

God saw Joseph in prison. He said, "I have a plan. Joseph is sad, but I will make him glad. He trusts in Me. I will make him glad. I have a plan."

> *Then Joseph's master took him*
> *and put him into the prison.*
> *(Genesis 39:20)*

Faith Lessons

Joseph did not sin — The man's wife **wanted** Joseph to sin. But Joseph did not sin. He said, "I will fear God. I will obey God. I must not sin." Do you fear God? Will you obey Him? Will you sin?

God has a plan — Joseph was very sad. He did not want to be a slave. He did not want to be in **prison**. But God had a plan. His plan is good.

Joseph can not see God's plan — God is very wise. Joseph can not see God's plan. But he can trust God. He can say, "God is wise. God is good. I will trust Him." Will you trust God?

Vocabulary

Egypt	obeyed	prison
trusted	wanted	
served	heard	

CHAPTER 10

Joseph is a Ruler

Joseph sat in prison. He did not want to be in prison. But he did not get mad. He said, "I will trust God."

Joseph was still a slave. He did good things in prison. He obeyed his **master**. The **master** told Joseph to help in the prison. Joseph did help.

Two men were in prison. The men had dreams. They told Joseph the dreams. Joseph said, "God can tell what a dream means."

The men heard Joseph. They said, "God is with

you. God gives you **wisdom**."

One day, the king of Egypt had a dream. He was **afraid**. He said, "What can this dream mean? I am **afraid** of my dream."

The wise men in Egypt did not help. They said, "We can not tell what this dream means."

But one man said, "Joseph can tell you what the dream means."

The king **called** Joseph. He **called** him out of prison. Joseph came to the king. The king told him his dream.

Joseph said, "God can tell you what the dream means." Joseph told the king his dream. "A **famine** will come on the land. Egypt will have no food. The **famine** will be long. It will be seven years long."

Joseph said, "God will give you food **before** the **famine**. You must keep this food. You must find a wise man to keep the food safe. Then all the people will have food to eat."

The king said, "You are a wise man. God is with you. I will make you a **ruler** in Egypt. You will keep Egypt safe in the **famine**."

Now Joseph is not a slave. Now he is a **ruler**. God **blessed** Joseph. He **ruled** in Egypt.

The **famine** came. There was no food. The brothers of Joseph had no food. They said, "There is food in Egypt. We will go to Egypt to get food."

The brothers came to Egypt. They bowed down to Joseph. They said, "Please give us food."

Joseph saw his brothers. His brothers were bad. His brothers hated Joseph. Will Joseph help his brothers?

Joseph said, "You hated me. You sold me as a slave. But I will love you. I will give you food."

Joseph gave his brothers food. He said, "I will not be mad. I will love you. I will keep you safe."

Did God have a plan? Yes, God had a plan. God sent Joseph to Egypt. He made Joseph a slave. Then He made Joseph a **ruler**. Now Joseph can keep his brothers safe. This is God's plan. It is a good plan. God is a good God.

But the LORD was with Joseph
and showed him mercy. (Genesis 39:21)

Faith Lessons

Joseph did not get mad — Joseph did not want to be in prison. His brothers did bad things to him. But he did not get mad. He trusted God. Do you get mad? We must not get mad. We must trust God.

Joseph loved his brothers — His brothers sinned. But Joseph still loved his brothers. He gave them food. He kept them safe. We must love like Joseph did.

Joseph is a picture of Jesus — The brothers were bad. But Joseph still loved them and helped them. He is a picture of Jesus. Jesus has a people just like Joseph had brothers. Jesus loves His people and saves them. His people sin, but Jesus will still love and save them.

Vocabulary

master	famine	ruled
wisdom	before	picture
afraid	ruler	
called	blessed	

CHAPTER 11

Israel Lives in Egypt

Joseph was in Egypt. His brothers came to Egypt for food. They told Jacob, "Joseph is in Egypt. He will give us food. He will keep us safe."

Jacob was glad. He said, "I will go to Egypt. I will see my son."

God said to Jacob, "I gave you a promise. I **promised** to give you a land. I will keep My promise. Go to Egypt. I will keep you safe there. I will give you **children**. I will keep your **children** safe. I will give them the land I **promised** you."

Jacob trusted God. God gave Jacob a new name. God called him Israel.

Jacob came to Egypt. He saw Joseph. He was glad. Joseph was glad. "God is good," Jacob said. "He has kept my son safe."

Jacob and his children lived in Egypt.

Jacob **grew** old. It was time for him to die. He told his sons, "God gave me a promise. He will give you a land. The land is not in Egypt. He will send you out of Egypt. He will give you a good land. You must trust God." Will Jacob's sons trust God?

Jacob **died**. Then his sons got old. His sons **died**.

The **children** of **Israel lived** in Egypt. They **lived** there for a long time. God blessed them. He gave them many boys and girls. They were called **Israelites**.

The **Israelites grew** and **grew**. They had lots and lots of **children**.

The king of Egypt saw this. He was afraid. He said, "The **Israelites** are strong. We must not let them be strong. We must make Egypt strong. We must make the **Israelites** weak."

The king made the people slaves. He did not want them to be strong. He made them **work** hard. He was a bad man. He did not like the Israelites.

The Israelites were sad. They did not want to be slaves. What did they do? They said, "We will pray. God will help us."

The people prayed to God. They said, "God, You

made a promise to Abraham. You made a promise to Isaac. You made a promise to Jacob. You **promised** to give us a land. Now we are slaves. We do not want to be slaves. Please help us. Please set us free. Please give us a land."

Did God hear the people pray? Yes, He did hear.

God made a promise. Will He keep His promise? Yes, He will keep it. The people can trust God.

Then the children of Israel groaned . . . and their cry came up to God.

(Exodus 2:23)

Faith Lessons

The king of Egypt sinned — The king of Egypt was afraid, so he sinned. We must not sin if we are afraid. We must trust God to keep us safe. We must not trust sin.

God will keep His promise — The Israelites prayed to God. They did ask Him to keep His promise. God will hear them pray. He will keep His promise. They can trust God. We can trust God, too.

Vocabulary

promised	lived	Israelites
children	grew	work
Israel	died	prayed

CHAPTER 12

Moses is Born

The Israelites grew in Egypt. The king of Egypt was afraid.

The king said, "I must keep Egypt strong. I will kill the **babies** of the Israelites. I will kill all the boys. I will make the Israelites weak."

The king **killed** the boy **babies** of Israel. Will he kill all the boy **babies**? No, he will not. God will save a boy.

A mom had a boy. She loved the boy. She said, "We must not let the king kill our baby. We will hide him."

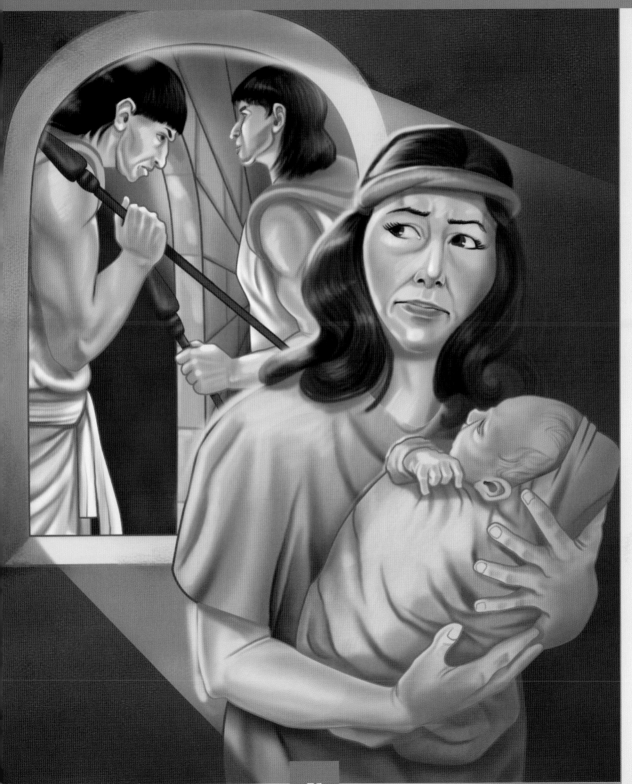

The mom hid her baby by the **river**. Will the king find her son? Will the king kill the baby?

A woman came to the **river**. The king of Egypt was her **father**. She saw the baby. Will she kill the baby? Will she tell her **father**? No, she will not. She said, "I will keep the baby. I will keep him safe."

She called the baby Moses. Moses grew up with the king of Egypt. Was Moses the son of the king? No, he was an Israelite.

Moses grew into a man. He said, "The king of Egypt has sinned. I will not sin with him. I will join the Israelites. They are my people. They are the people of God. I will serve God."

Moses saw his people. The Israelites were slaves. They were very sad. The king of Egypt did bad things to them.

God told Moses, "I will save My people. I will save them from the king of Egypt. I hear them pray. I see they are sad. I will save them." How will God save them?

God said, "I made a promise. I will give them a land. I will keep My promise."

God said to Moses, "I will send you to the king. You will bring My people away from Egypt. You will bring them to a land I will give you."

Moses was afraid. He said, "I am weak. The king of Egypt is strong. I am afraid to talk to him."

But God said, "I made you. I made the king. I made all things. Do not be afraid of the king. I will be with you. Do not be afraid."

Was Moses afraid? Yes, he was afraid. But Moses trusted God. He said, "I will do what God tells me to do. God is strong. I will fear Him. I will not fear the king. I will trust God."

"I will send you to Pharaoh that you may bring My people, the children of Israel, out of Egypt."
(Exodus 3:10)

Faith Lessons

A mom trusted God — A mom had a baby boy. She did not want the king to kill her baby. She trusted God. She said, "God can save my baby." Do you trust God?

God is a strong God — Egypt was a strong land. Its king was a strong king. But God was stronger. God is stronger than all kings. He is stronger than all lands. He is a strong God.

God made all things — Moses was afraid. He was weak, and the king was strong. But God said, "Do not be afraid." God made all things. He is stronger than all things. We do not need to be afraid. We must trust God when we are afraid.

God will save His people — The Israelites were slaves. But God said, "I will save them." Are you a slave? Yes, you are a slave to sin. Can God save you from your sins? Yes, He can. God can save from sin.

Vocabulary

babies	father	trusted
killed	Moses	stronger
river	talk	

CHAPTER 13

God Saves at the Red Sea

Moses went to the king of Egypt. He said, "You must let the people go. You must not make them slaves. You must obey God."

The king said, "I will not obey God. I do not fear God. I am strong. I will keep the people slaves." Will the king win?

God said, "The king of Egypt will not fear Me. I will **punish** the king."

Did God **punish** the king? Yes, He did. God killed the cows in Egypt. He sent **hail**. The **hail** killed the plants in Egypt. Now the people of Egypt had no food.

God said, "I will **punish** Egypt. I will teach the king to fear Me. Then I will let My people go free."

God sent an **angel**. The **angel** killed the sons in Egypt.

The king of Egypt was afraid. He said, "The God of Moses will kill me. He will kill Egypt. I must let the Israelites go. I must not make them slaves."

The king said to Moses, "Take the people and go away."

Now the Israelites were glad. Now they were not slaves. They said, "God is strong. We will not fear the king."

God led the people out of Egypt. He said, "I will give you a good land to live in. Obey Me, and I will give you a land."

The people were glad. They **followed** God. They

followed Moses.

The people left Egypt. They said, "We will go to the land God gave us." But they can not cross the Red Sea. The Red Sea is big. It is deep. It has lots of water. They can not cross.

The king of Egypt got mad. He said, "I will kill the Israelites. I will kill them at the Red Sea." He called his men. The king and his men chased the people.

The people are stuck at the Red Sea. They can not cross the sea.

The people are afraid of the king. They are afraid of his men. They tell Moses, "We are stuck! The king will kill us!"

Did the people trust God? No, they did not trust Him. They are afraid of the king.

Moses said, "Do not be afraid. God will keep us safe."

God sent a wind. The wind pushed the water away.

The **Red Sea** was **dry**. Now the people can cross the sea on **dry** land.

The king saw the water. He saw the **dry** land. He said, "I will cross on the **dry** land, too. I will kill the people."

The king and his men came to the **Red Sea**. They went on the **dry** land.

But God said, "I will bring the water back. It will kill the men of Egypt."

The water came back. It killed the king and his men.

Now the Israelites are glad. They sing to God. God will keep them safe.

Say to the children of Israel: "I am the Lord; I will bring you out . . . and I will redeem you."
(Exodus 6:6)

Faith Lessons

God will punish sin — The king of Egypt sinned. God said, "I will **punish** you for your sin." God must **punish** for sin.

Moses feared and trusted God — Moses feared God. This means he trusted God. He did what God said. He was not afraid of the king of Egypt. We must not be afraid of bad things. We must fear God.

God saved His people at the Red Sea — The people were afraid. They said, "We can not cross the sea!" But God saved them. He is strong. He is wise. He will save His people.

Vocabulary

punish	followed	pushed
hail	Red Sea	dry
angel	chased	

CHAPTER 14

God Sends Manna

God saved the people of Israel. He killed the king of Egypt. He killed his men. Now the Israelites are safe. Will they trust God now?

Moses led the people. He will lead them to the land God will give them.

The people **walked** and **walked**. It was a long walk. They got **tired**. They said, "We are in a **desert**!"

The people started to **whine**. They said, "God will not keep us safe. We will die here in the **desert**."

Moses said, "Do not **whine**. Do not be afraid. God

will lead us. He will keep us safe."

The people do not trust God. They do not trust Moses. They got mad at Moses. They said, "We are in a **desert**! Will you give us food? What will we eat? We will go back to Egypt. We will find food there."

Did the people trust God? No, they did not trust God. They got mad at God.

God **heard** the people **whine**. He said, "The people do not trust Me. They do not obey Me. But I will have **mercy** on them. I will give them food."

God said to Moses, "Tell the people I will give them food."

The people went to bed. When they woke up, they saw a white thing on the **ground**. They said, "What is it?"

Moses said, "God will give you food. This white thing is food for you."

The people took the white thing. They ate it. It was

good. It was sweet. They said, "We like this food."

The people said, "We will call this food Manna."

God sent manna to the people. He said, "I will give
you manna. Every day, when you wake up, you will

find manna. I will send it to you to eat."

God is good to the people. He gave them food to eat. Will the people trust God now?

God will test the people. He said, "I will send the manna every day. But on the Sabbath day, I will not send it. You must keep some manna for the Sabbath day. Then you will have food to eat on every day."

Did the people obey God? No, they did not obey Him. On the Sabbath day, they woke up. They went to get the manna. But the manna was not there.

God said, "You must obey Me. You must not work on the Sabbath day. You must rest on this day."

Will the people obey God now? Will they trust Him? Wait and see.

And the house of Israel called its name Manna.

(Exodus 16:31)

Faith Lessons

The people got tired and whined — The people got tired. They whined to Moses. It is not good to whine. God will give us what we need. We must trust in Him. We must be glad for what we have. We must not whine.

God has mercy — The people did not trust God. But God said, "I will have mercy." God is a good God. He is a God of mercy.

God is good — The people whined. They did not trust God. But God will still give them food. Do you whine? Do you sin? We do sin. But God still gives us food. He is a very good God. We must love Him.

Vocabulary

walked	whine	ground
tired	heard	manna
desert	mercy	Sabbath

CHAPTER 15

The Ten Commandments

God gave food to the Israelites. The people ate the manna. But the people did not trust God. They did not obey God.

God said, "I will teach you to obey. I will give you a law. My law will be a good law. It will teach you what is good. It will teach you what is bad."

God is a good God. He will give His people a good law. A good law keeps people safe. It will teach them what is good. It will teach them how to obey. God's law is good for His people.

God said, "I am the **Lord** God. I saved you from the king of Egypt. You were a slave. But I saved you. Obey Me and keep My **law**."

God gave His people ten **laws**. He said:

1. "I am your God. Do not **worship** any **other** god. Trust in Me. Do not trust in **other** gods."

2. "Do not make a **picture** of Me. Do not **worship** any **other** thing. You must **worship** Me in the way I tell you. Do not **worship** Me any **other** way."

3. "**Respect** My name. Do not say My name in fun."

4. "Keep the Sabbath day. Do not work on this day. Rest on this day."

5. "**Respect** your dad and mom. Obey them."

6. "Do not kill a person. **Protect** the life of **other** people."

7. "Moms and dads make a promise when they **marry**. Do not **break** this promise. You must keep it."

8. "Do not steal."

9. "Do not lie."

10. "Be glad for what you have. Do not want what other people have."

The people heard God speak. They heard God give His law. They were afraid of God. Will they obey God's law?

Do you obey God's law? Do you do what is good?

We all sin. We must try to obey God's law. But we will sin. Can we stop all our sin? No, we can not stop it.

God said, "My people sin. But I will save them from sin. I will send My Son. He is the Seed I promised. He will save His people from sin."

God is a good God. He gives us a good law. And He will save His people from sin.

"I am the Lord *your God . . . You shall have no other gods before Me."*
(Deuteronomy 5:6-7)

Faith Lessons

God gave a law — God gives us a good law. We must obey God. We must obey His law. God promises to bless us when we keep His law. Bad things happen when we do not keep this law.

God's law will teach us — God's law will teach us what is good. It will teach us what is bad. It will teach us what God is like.

God will save from sin — The people of God sinned. They did not obey God. I sin. You sin. We do not obey God. We can not obey His law. We must pray to God. We must trust Him. He is a good God. He will save His people from sin.

Vocabulary

law	other	protect
lord	picture	marry
worship	respect	break

CHAPTER 16

Twelve Men Look at the Good Land

oses led the people in the desert. They walked and walked. It was a long way.

God said, "I made a promise to Abraham. I promised to give him a land. I will keep My promise. I will give you a land."

God led the people to the land.

God said to Moses, "Tell 12 men to go into the land. Tell them to look at the land. Tell them to look at the people. It is a good land. I will give you this land."

God said, "Bad people live in this land. But do not be afraid of them. I will give you the land. I made a promise. I will keep My promise."

Moses sent 12 men. Two of the men were Caleb

and Joshua. Moses told them, "Go into the land. Look at the land. Be brave and see what the land is like."

Did the men obey? Yes, they did obey. The men went to the land God gave them. They saw the land. They saw the people in the land. The people were big. The people were strong. The people had houses. The houses were strong.

The men came back to Moses. They told Moses, "We went to the land. We saw the people in the land. The people are big. They are so big that we are like bugs. The people are strong. They are stronger than we are."

The Israelites heard what the men said. Then they began to cry.

Why did the people cry? They were afraid. They said, "The people in the land will kill us. We will die. Our kids will die. We will all die. This is not a good land! This is a bad land!"

But **Caleb** and **Joshua** said, "Do not **cry**! The land is a good land. It is a very good land. God is strong. He will give us the land. He will not let us die. We must obey God. Do not be afraid. Do not **cry**."

Did the people like what **Caleb** and **Joshua** said? No, they did not like it. They said, "Kill **Caleb**! Kill **Joshua**! They say bad things! God is not strong. He will not save us. We will go back to Egypt. We will be safe in Egypt."

Did the people trust God? No, they did not trust Him.

God **heard** the people. God was **angry**. He said, "You did not trust Me. You did not obey Me. I will not give you the land. I will punish you for your sin. You will not go into the land. You will die in the desert."

Will God **forget** His promise? No, He will not **forget**.

God said, "**Caleb** and **Joshua** obeyed Me. They

trusted Me. I will give them the land. They will not die. They will live. I will bless them. They will live in the good land I give them."

"He will bring us into this land and give it to us, . . .
the LORD is with us. Do not fear them."
(Numbers 14:8-9)

Faith Lessons

The people did not trust God — The people were afraid. Why were they afraid? Why did they **cry**? They did not trust God. We do not have to be afraid. We do not have to **cry**. We must trust God. He is good.

Caleb and Joshua obeyed God — The people were afraid. Did **Caleb** and **Joshua listen** to the people? No, they did not. They said, "We will **listen** to God. God is strong. We will **listen** to Him." We must not **listen** to bad things people say. We must listen to God.

God will not forget His promise — The people sinned. They did not trust God. God will punish them for this sin. But He will not **forget** His promise. He will still have mercy. He will still keep His promise.

Vocabulary

Caleb	heard	angry
Joshua	began	forget
house	cry	listen

CHAPTER 17

The Song of Moses

God said to Moses, "The people will not come into My land. They did not obey Me. They will live in the desert 40 **years**. They will die in the desert. Then I will bring **their** children into the land."

Moses told the people what God said. The people were very sad. They did not trust God. They were afraid. This made them sad.

Moses said, "God is like a rock. He is strong. He is good. But you have sinned. You did not trust God."

Moses said, "You must **learn** to trust God. You must **re-mem-ber** what God did for you."

Moses told the people, "God made a promise to Abraham. God kept His promise. Then God made a promise to Isaac. He made a promise to Jacob."

Then Moses said, "Do you **remember**? God saved Joseph when he was a slave. God made him a **ruler**. God **blessed** him. Joseph obeyed God. Joseph trusted God."

Moses told the people, "Joseph died. Then the king of Egypt made us slaves. We did not want to be slaves. What did God do? Do you **remember**? God saved us. God killed the king and his men. God set us free."

Moses said, "God led us in the desert. We had no food. Did God forget us? No, He did not forget! He sent manna. We ate the manna. God kept us safe."

Then Moses said, "God is a good God. He gave us a law. His law is good. His law will help us. It will teach

us what is good and what is bad. Do you remember
His law? Do you remember that God is good?"

Moses said, "God has a land. It is a good land. He
will not give you the land. You sinned. You did not

obey. God will not let you come into the land. But He will give the land to your children. Your children must not be afraid. They must trust God. They must fear God. They must love God. They must **remember** what God did."

Moses said, "You must teach your children. Tell them, 'Do not forget.' Do not forget God. Do not forget what God did for you."

Then Moses said, "I will **praise** God. I will sing to Him. He is a good God. He is a God of mercy. I will **remember** my God. I will **remember** His mercy. I will trust in Him."

Then Moses spoke . . . the words of this song until they were ended.
(Deuteronomy 31:30)

Faith Lessons

God has mercy on us — The people sinned. God said, "You will not come into the land. You will die in the desert." But God had mercy. God let **their** children come into the land. We sin, too. But God has mercy on us.

Remember what God did — God made us. He gave us a mom and a dad. He keeps us safe. We must **remember** what God did for us. We must **remember** what He did for Israel. We must praise Him. He is a very good God.

Vocabulary

year	remember	praise
their	ruler	
learn	blessed	

CHAPTER 18

The Fall of Jericho

Moses was old. God told him, "You will die. Tell Joshua to lead the people. Joshua will lead the people into the land I give them." Moses told Joshua. Then Moses died.

God said to Joshua, "You will lead My people. Do not be afraid. You will go into the land. Do not be afraid of the strong bad men. You must be brave. Trust in Me. Do not fear."

Will Joshua be afraid? Will he trust God?

God said, "I will be with you. You will not be

alone. I will help you. I will **fight** for you. You will win. Do not be afraid."

Joshua led the people. The people went into the land. They came to a big **city**. The **city** was **Jericho**. The **city** had big walls. Can Joshua **fight** the people in the **city**? No, he cannot. He cannot get up the walls.

God told Joshua, "I will give you **Jericho**. Call the Israelites. Tell them to walk **around** the **city**. Tell them to walk **around** the walls. They will walk **around** the **city** for seven days. Then I will give you **Jericho**. The bad men will not win. You will win."

Joshua **called** the people. He said, "God will give us the **city**. But we must obey God. We must walk **around** the **city**. For seven days we will walk **around** the **city**."

The people said, "We will obey God. We will follow you. We will do what God says."

The people walked **around Jericho**. They walked

around it one day. Then they walked around it two days. For seven days they walked around the city.

On the seventh day, Joshua said, "Shout! The Lord has given you the city. Trust Him. Be brave. Go take the city!"

The people gave a shout. They were glad. Then God broke down the walls of Jericho. The walls fell down flat.

The people of Israel went into the city. Did they win the fight? Yes, they did win. God gave them the city.

The people will praise God. They will thank Him. He is a strong God. He will fight for His people. He will keep them safe. He will let them win. He will keep His promise. He will give them the land.

The people shouted with a great shout, [and] the wall fell down flat.

(Joshua 6:20)

Faith Lessons

We must trust God — Joshua saw Jericho. It was a big city. It was a bad city. But Joshua was not afraid. He was brave. He trusted in God. We see bad things. We see bad people. But we must not be afraid. We must trust in God.

The people praised God — God gave His people the city. He kept His people safe. The people praised God. Did they thank Him? Yes, they did. We must praise God. We must thank Him, too.

Vocabulary

alone	Jericho	seventh
fight	around	shout
city	called	thank

CHAPTER 19

God Speaks to Gideon

Joshua was a good man. He trusted God. He obeyed God. But Joshua died. Then the Israelites did not trust God. They did not obey Him. They did not do what was **right**. They served bad gods.

God said, "My people have sinned. I will punish My people. I will send bad men to **fight** them. Then My people will pray. They will be sad for **their** sin."

God sent bad men. The men were from **Midian**. The bad men were strong. They stole from the Israelites. They took **their** food. They took **their** sheep. They took **their** stuff.

The Israelites were sad. They were afraid. They said, "We will pray to God. God is strong. He can save us."

God heard them pray. He said, "I will save them. I will pick a man to **fight Midian**."

God saw a man. The man was **Gideon**. God said to **Gideon**, "The Lord is with you. You are a strong man. You are a man of **might**."

Gideon heard God speak. He was afraid. He said, "I am not strong. The bad men of **Midian** are strong."

But God said, "I will be with you. I will help you **fight**. Do not be afraid of **Midian**."

Then God said, "My people have sinned. They trust in bad gods. See this house for **their** bad god? You must **tear** down this house."

Gideon was afraid. The people **might** see him **tear** down the house. They **might** be angry. They **might** kill him. **Gideon** said, "I will **tear** down the house at night. They will not see me."

Gideon obeyed God. But he was afraid. He broke down the house of the bad god. He did it at night. There was no light. No one saw him.

The next day, the people got mad. "Who broke down the house of our god?" they said.

A man said, "Gideon did it."

The people got very mad. They said, "We will kill Gideon!" But God kept Gideon safe.

God said, "Gideon, you are a man of might. I will make you strong. You will fight Midian. You will win. I will be with you. I will be your God."

Is Gideon afraid? Yes, he is afraid. Will Gideon trust God? Yes, he will trust Him. God will make him strong. God will win the fight.

> "Go in this might of yours, and you shall save Israel from the hand of the Midianites. Have I not sent you?"
>
> (Judges 6:14)

Faith Lessons

God speaks to us — God spoke to Gideon. Will God speak to us, too? Yes, He will. He will speak to us in His Word. He will speak to us in the **Bible**. The **Bible** is His letter to us. We must read it. We must obey it.

Gideon obeyed — Gideon was afraid, but he still obeyed God. He did what God told him to do. The people were mad. They said, "We will kill Gideon!" But Gideon still obeyed God. We must obey God. If people get mad, we must still obey God.

God was with Gideon — Gideon was afraid, but God was still with him. God is with us when we are afraid, too.

Vocabulary

right	Gideon	light
fight	might	Bible
their	tear	
Midian	night	

CHAPTER 20

God Helps Gideon Win

Gideon was not a strong man. But he trusted God. God made him strong.

Gideon said to Israel, "Let us fight Midian. God will fight with us. We will win."

The people came to Gideon. They said, "We will fight with you. We will win."

Many men came to Gideon. God saw the men that came. He said, "There are too many men. If they win, they will say, 'We are strong. That is why we win.' They will not trust Me. They think they are strong."

God said, "I do not want many men. I will pick some men. I will not pick many. You can send the rest home. I want the men to trust in Me."

Gideon said to the men, "Are you afraid? If you are afraid, please go home. We do not need many men. God will fight for us."

Many men were afraid. They did not want to fight. Gideon sent them home.

Then God said, "You still have too many men. Bring the men to a river. Let them drink. I will pick some men at the river."

Gideon obeyed God. He led the men to a river. God picked 300 men. Gideon sent the rest of the men home. Now he did not have many men left.

Midian had many men. They had lots and lots of men. But Gideon had 300 men. He did not have many men at all. Was he afraid? Yes, he was afraid. But he trusted God. "God is strong," he said. "I do not need many men. God will fight for me."

At night, God said to Gideon, "Go to the army of Midian. Do not fight. Stand still, and I will fight for you."

Gideon led his men at night. They went to the army of Midian. It was dark. There was no light. Gideon told his men, "Shout and shine your light."

The men did shout. They held up a light.

The army of Midian heard the shout. They saw the light. They said, "A big army is here! It will kill us!" They were afraid. God made them afraid. They did not fight Gideon. They ran away.

Gideon chased them. Gideon and his men killed the army of Midian.

Gideon had 300 men. He did not have a big army. But God was with him. God was stronger than Midian. God let Gideon win.

And the LORD said to Gideon, "The people who are with you are too many."

(Judges 7:2)

Faith Lessons

God will help His people — The army of Midian was big. It was strong. But God said, "I will help My people. I will save them from Midian." God is good to His people. He will help them.

God is strong. We are not — Gideon did not have many men. Why did he win? His men were not strong. But God is strong. Gideon obeyed God. He trusted God, and God will fight for Gideon. That is why Gideon will win. We must remember that we are not strong. God is strong. We must trust Him. We must thank Him.

God will save His people — Midian was a strong enemy. Gideon was not strong. But God saved the people of Israel. Sin is a strong enemy just like Midian. We can not fight sin and win. We are not strong. But God is strong. He will fight for His people. He will save His people from sin just like He saved Gideon and Israel.

Vocabulary

many	river	army
why	drink	enemy
think	picked	

CHAPTER 21

God Gives Hannah a Son

One day, a man came to **worship** God. The man lived in Israel. He had a wife. And he came to **worship** God. He went to the house of God in Israel.

But the man had a **problem**. He did not have one wife. He had two. It is not good to have two wives.

One wife was **proud**. She had children. She said, "I am a good wife. I have children." She did not like the **other** wife. She was not nice to the **other** wife.

The **other** wife did not have children. Her name

was Hannah. Hannah was sad.

The man told Hannah, "Do not be sad." But she was still sad.

Hannah said, "I will pray to God. God will hear me."

Hannah went to pray to God. She was very sad. She cried and prayed. She said, "God, please give me a son. If You give me a son, I will give him to You. My son will serve You all his life. He will live in Your house and he will serve You."

Hannah prayed and prayed. Did God hear her pray? Yes, He did.

Then Hannah went home. She said, "I will not be sad. I will wait. God will hear my prayer."

God did hear her pray. God sent her a son. Hannah loved her son. She named him Samuel.

Then Hannah said, "I love Samuel. God heard me and gave me a son. I love my son. But now I will give my son to God."

Hannah took Samuel to the house of God in Israel. She gave him to a man at the house. She said, "This is my son. God gave me a son. Now I will give my son to God."

The man took Samuel. He said to Hannah, "God will keep your son. Your son will stay at God's house. He will serve God."

Samuel lived at the house of God. He helped at the house. He obeyed the man at the house of God.

Hannah loved Samuel. She made him a coat. Every year she came to see Samuel. She gave him a new coat.

God blessed Hannah. He gave her more children. She had five children. She was glad. She was glad to have children. She was glad to have Samuel.

She said, "I will praise God. God is good to me."

She said, "God is strong. He can kill. He can make

alive. He will save His people. He will keep His people safe. God is good to me. He is good to His people."

[Hannah] called his name Samuel, saying, "Because I have asked for him from the LORD."

(1 Samuel 1:20)

Faith Lessons

Hannah was sad, so she prayed — Hannah was sad. She did not have a son. She cried. Then she prayed. We must pray to God when we are sad. We must trust Him.

God made the world — Hannah did not have a son. Did she want a son? Yes, she did. Can she make a son? No, she cannot make a son. But God can make a son. God made all things. He can make a son for Hannah. God is strong.

Hannah will praise God — God gave Hannah a son. Then Hannah said, "I will praise God." It is good to sing praise to God. It is good to thank God. He is a good God. Let us praise Him!

Vocabulary

worship	other	took
problem	Hannah	
proud	Samuel	

CHAPTER 22

God Picks David to Be King

Samuel grew up. Now he is not a boy. Now he is a man. He is a man of God. He is a prophet. A prophet will speak the word of God. He will tell people what God says to them.

God said to Samuel, "I will pick a man to be king. He will be a king for Israel. He will rule My people. He will be a good king."

God sent Samuel to find the king. He said, "Go to the house of Jesse. I will pick a king. He will be one of the sons of Jesse."

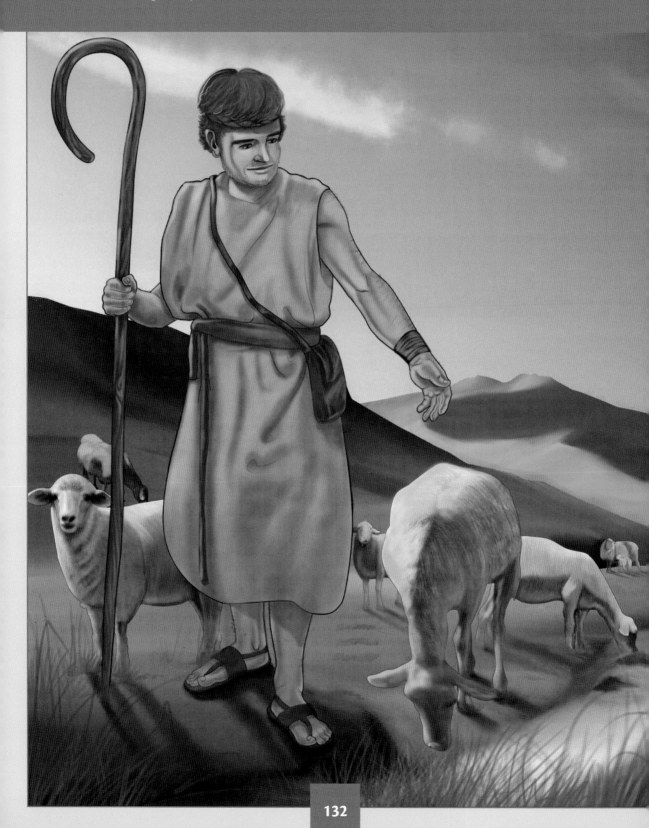

Samuel went to the house of Jesse. He said, "I want to see your sons."

Jesse showed Samuel his sons. Samuel saw a son. He said, "This man is big. He is strong. God will pick this man!"

But God said, "I will not pick this man. I do not want a big man. I want a man who will love Me. I want a man who will obey Me. I want a man who will trust Me."

Jesse called his sons. Samuel saw the sons of Jesse. His sons were big.

They were strong. But Samuel said, "God did not pick these sons."

Then Jesse said, "One son is not here. He is in the field. He is with the sheep."

Samuel said, "Call him."

Jesse called his son. The son's name was David. Will God pick David?

Samuel saw David. Then God told Samuel, "This is the right son. He will be king."

Samuel said, "David, you will be a king. God will make you a king. You must serve God. You must obey God. You must fear God. You must love Him."

Will David serve God? Will he obey? Will he love God? Wait and see.

David will be king one day. But he is not king yet. Israel has a king. The king's name is Saul.

When will David be king? He must wait. He will wait. One day God will make him a king just like

Samuel said. **David** will wait for God to make him king.

> *"For the LORD does not see as man sees; . . .*
>
> *the LORD looks at the heart."*
>
> *(1 Samuel 16:7)*

Faith Lessons

God will pick a man who loves Him — The sons of Jesse were big. They were strong. But God did not pick them. Why? He said, "I do not want a big man. I want a man who will fear Me. I want a man who will obey Me. I want a man who will love Me."

David will wait for God — God said, "I will make David king." But David is not king yet. Will David trust God? Yes, he will. He will trust God and he will wait. God will make him king one day. God will keep His promise. But David must wait for God.

We must wait for God to keep His promise — Jesus made a promise. He said He will come back. One day He will come back to judge the world. We must trust Him. And we must wait for Him to keep His promise.

Vocabulary

prophet	called	David
Jesse	these	Saul
showed	field	judge

CHAPTER 23

David Fights Goliath

Bad men came to fight Israel. The men were **Philistines**. Saul was king of Israel. He called his army and went to fight. But his army was afraid. The **Philistines** were strong. They had a big man. The man was a **giant**. His name was **Goliath**.

Goliath said, "I will fight you! I will kill you!"

The people were afraid to fight **Goliath**. They said, "He will kill us! We will not fight him!"

King Saul was sad. The people were sad. Who can save them from **Goliath**?

David was not with the army. He was with the sheep. He kept the sheep safe. Then his dad said, "Go to the army of Israel. Go see your brothers. See if they are well."

David went to the army. He **found** his brothers. Then he heard a **sound**. What was the **sound**? It was **Goliath**.

Goliath said, "You will not fight me. You are not brave. You are not strong. Your God is not strong. Your God is weak. You are afraid to fight!"

David heard **Goliath** speak. David got mad. He said, "This man is very bad. He says bad things. I will fight him."

King Saul heard David. He said, "You cannot fight **Goliath**. He is too big. He is too strong."

But David said, "I am not strong like **Goliath**. But God is strong. God will fight with me. **Goliath** is a bad man. He says bad things. God will kill **Goliath**. I

am not afraid. I will trust in God."

Then David looked around. He found a round stone. He had a sling. He said, "I will kill Goliath with my sling and a stone."

David went to meet **Goliath**. **Goliath** looked **around**. He saw David. He saw David's sling and stone. He said, "Am I a dog? Will you fight me with a stick or a stone? Come here, and I will kill you!"

But David said, "You are big. You are strong. But you say God is not good. You say bad things. God will fight for me. I fight in the name of the Lord God. The Lord God will kill you."

Then David took his sling. He took his stone. He hit **Goliath** with the stone. Then the **giant** fell to the **ground**. David killed him on the **ground**.

The **Philistines** saw what David did. Now they were afraid. They ran away. They did not want to fight. They said, "God is a strong God. We will not fight Him!"

But David fights. The men of Israel fight. They are not afraid. Now they are brave. God will fight for them.

"I will strike you and take your head from you . . .

that all the earth may know that there is a

God in Israel."

(1 Samuel 17:46)

Faith Lessons

David was not afraid — Goliath was a very big man. He was a giant! But David did not fear him. He said, "I will not fear this big man. I will fear God. God is stronger than this man." We must fear God, too.

God saved Israel — The men of Israel were afraid. But God said, "I will save Israel. I will let David fight the giant. I will kill Goliath." God saved Israel from the Philistines. We must trust in God. He is strong. He can save us, too.

Vocabulary

Philistines	found	round
giant	sound	ground
Goliath	around	

CHAPTER 24

David is King

Saul was king of Israel. But Saul was not a good man. He did not fear God. He did not obey God's law. He was a **wicked** man.

God told Samuel, "Saul will not obey Me. He will not obey My law. I will not let him be king."

Samuel was **sorry** to hear this. He was **sorry** that Saul was **wicked**. He told Saul, "You did not obey the word of the Lord. God will not let you be king. He will take the **kingdom** away from you. He will give the **kingdom** to a new king."

Saul was sad. He was **sorry**, too. But he did not trust God. He got angry. He said, "God will make David king. But I will kill David!"

Saul sent men to kill David. Then he said, "I will hunt for David. I will find him and kill him." But did Saul find David? Did he kill him? No, he did not. God kept David safe. God did not let Saul kill David.

Then God sent the Philistines. They came to fight Israel. Saul called his army. He led his army to fight the Philistines. Will Saul win the **battle**?

Saul is afraid. He is afraid to die. Will he die in the **battle**?

The Philistines come to fight. The Israelites come to fight. They fight a big **battle**. Many people die. But the Philistines win the **battle**. Saul is killed. His sons are killed. Now Israel has no king.

What will Israel do?

The people called David. They said, "Come be our

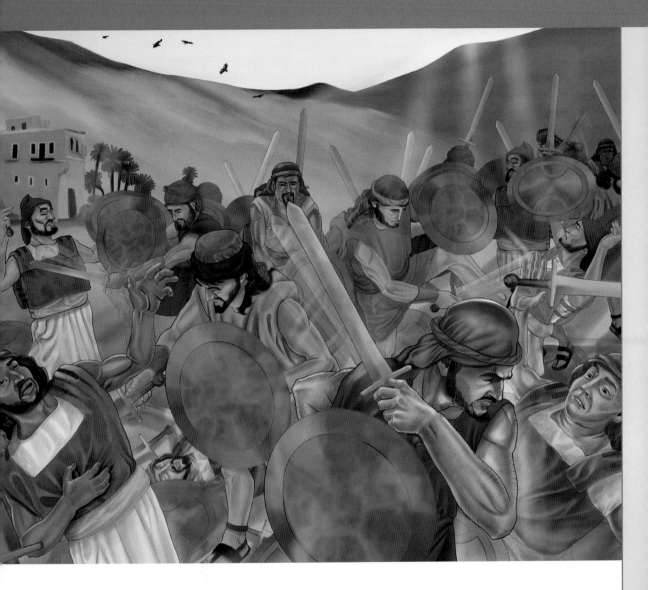

new king. You will be a good king for Israel."

Will David come? Yes, he will come. Now he will be king of Israel.

David said, "God made a promise. He promised to

make me king. Now He has kept His promise. Now I am king. I will praise the Lord."

Then David sang a song to the Lord. He said, "The Lord is my Rock. He has saved me from my enemy. He kept me safe. He did not let Saul kill me."

David sang, "I will praise the Lord. He is good. I will follow Him. I will keep His law. I will not forget His word. God is full of mercy. He will have mercy on me."

I will love You, O Lord, my strength.

The Lord is my rock.

(Psalm 18:1-2)

Faith Lessons

Saul did not fear God — Saul did not obey God. When he sinned, he did not pray to God. Saul was angry at God. He did not trust God. We must not be like Saul. We must not be angry at God. We must trust Him. We must pray to Him when we sin.

God will punish for sin — Saul did not obey God. God said, "I must punish for sin, so I will punish Saul for his sin." God will punish all the world for sin. One day Jesus will come and punish the world for sin.

David praised God — God kept His promise to David. This made David glad. He praised God. He thanked God. We must praise God, too.

God is full of mercy — God did not let Saul kill David. God kept David safe. He is a God of mercy. He will have mercy on His people. We must thank God for His mercy.

Vocabulary

wicked	kingdom	enemy
sorry	battle	thanked

CHAPTER 25

God's Covenant with David

David was king. Now he had to fight the Philistines. **Could** he win? Saul did not win. **Could** David win?

David prayed. He **asked** God, "**Should** I go fight the Philistines? Will I win?"

The Lord said, "Go and fight the Philistines. I will fight with you. I will let you win."

David called his army. The men of Israel came. David led them to battle. **Would** David trust God? Yes, he **would**!

God let David win. He beat the Philistines.

David was a strong king. Now he had a strong kingdom.

God had a plan for David. He said, "David, when

you were a boy, you kept sheep safe. You lived with the sheep and kept watch on them. When you were a boy, I kept you safe.

"Now you are a man. Now you are a king. Who made you a king? I did. I kept you safe from Saul. I did not let Saul kill you. I made you king of Israel."

God said, "I kept you safe from the Philistines. I will stop all your enemies. I will not let your enemies hurt you. I am your God, and I will keep you safe."

Then God said, "I promised to give a land to My people. Now they live in the land I gave them. I kept My promise. Now I will make a promise with you. I made you king. And I will make your sons kings, too. This is My promise."

God made a promise with David. This promise is called a cov-e-nant.

God said, "I will set up your throne forever. I will send a King who will rule forever. The King will come from your family. He will be a good King. He will rule **forever**."

David heard what God said. Then David said, "God, I am a man. I sin just like all people sin. I do not **deserve** the promise You gave me. I do not **deserve** Your love. You are a God of mercy. I do not **deserve** Your mercy."

Then David said, "I will praise the Lord. He is God, and His words are true. He will bless His people. He will keep His **covenant forever**!"

"And now, O Lord God, You are God, and Your words are true, and You have promised this goodness to Your servant."

(2 Samuel 7:28)

Faith Lessons

God chose David to be king — David was a man just like us. He sinned just like us. But God still chose him. God had mercy and chose a sinful man. Praise God for His mercy!

God will send a King — God promised to send a King. This King will rule forever. Who is this King? He is Jesus Christ. He is ruling and He will rule forever! Thank God for this King!

Jesus has a kingdom — God gave David a kingdom. He ruled the land of Israel. But Jesus has a bigger kingdom. He rules all the world! His kingdom fills all lands. It rules all people. And it will last forever.

Vocabulary

could	would	covenant
asked	watch	forever
should	enemies	deserve

CHAPTER 26

David is Kind to Mephibosheth

D avid was king of Israel. He was a strong king. But he was a good king, too.

Saul died in the battle. His sons had died. But Saul's family did not die.

David said, "Saul was a bad king. Saul tried to kill me. But I will not be angry. I will not be angry at Saul's family."

David had a friend. The friend was Saul's son. The son died in the battle. But David did not forget his friend. He said, "I will be kind to the family of Saul. I will be kind to my friend's family."

But how can David be kind?

David sent for a man. He said, "Is Saul's family still alive? Can I help them? I want to be kind to them."

The man said, "One man is still alive. His name is Me-phi-bo-sheth. He is lame. His legs are hurt. He cannot walk."

David told the man, "Bring him here to me."

The man called Mephibosheth. But Mephibosheth was afraid. He said, "Will King David kill me? I am from Saul's family. Is David angry at Saul's family? Will he kill me?"

Mephibosheth was not strong. He was weak. Can he fight David? No, he cannot. He cannot even walk!

Mephibosheth came to David. He said, "David can kill me. But I cannot fight. I am weak."

Mephibosheth fell down in front of David. He bowed down to the ground. He said, "I am your

slave."

But David said, "No. Do not be afraid. I am not angry. I will not **hurt** you. I will be kind to you. I will love you. I will keep you safe."

David gave **Mephibosheth** land. He gave him food. He said, "You will live in the **palace** with me. You will be like my son."

David loved **Mephibosheth**. He did not hate him. He did not hate the **family** of Saul. David was kind to Saul's **family**. He said, "I will love Saul's **family**. I will love them just like God loved me."

David was a good king.

Then the king said,
"Is there not still someone of the house of Saul,
to whom I may show the kindness of God?"
(2 Samuel 9:3)

Faith Lessons

God loves His people — God sees His people. His people sin. I sin. You sin. We all sin. But God loves His people. He will **forgive** their sin. He will save His people, and He will love them.

David loved Mephibosheth — God made David king. David said, "God loves me. Now I will love others. God teaches me to love." We must love like David did. We must see how God loves us. We must thank God for His love. Then we must love others, too.

Jesus is the best King — David was a good king. He loved Mephibosheth. But David was not the best king. Who was? David is a picture of Jesus. Jesus is a very good King. He is the best King. He loves His people. And He will love them forever.

We are like Mephibosheth — We are not strong. We are weak like Mephibosheth. Sin makes us weak. And we cannot get well. We cannot fight sin. But God has mercy on us. He sees we are weak, and He says, "I will be strong for you. I will fight sin. I will win. I will save you from sin."

Vocabulary

family	Mephibosheth	palace
friend	lame	forgive
alive	hurt	

CHAPTER 27

Birds Bring Food to Elijah

David was a good king. But he grew old and died. Then other kings ruled Israel. Some kings were good. Some were bad. One bad king was Ahab. He was a very wicked man. He did not fear God. He did not serve God. He served idols.

The people of Israel followed Ahab. They did not follow God. They served Ahab's idols, too.

God saw wicked Ahab. He saw the wicked Israelites. He said, "I will judge Ahab. I will judge Israel. I will punish them for their sins."

God called a man. The man was Elijah. Elijah was a prophet. He spoke God's word to the people. God gave Elijah a message. The message was for King Ahab.

Elijah told Ahab, "God will judge you for your sins. He will judge the people for their sins. God will stop the rain. It will not rain on the land at all."

Did the word of God come true? Yes, it did. The rain did not fall on Israel for three years. All the plants died. All the crops died. A famine came to the land. The people had no food. The animals had no food. The people of Israel were very hungry.

God told Elijah, "Go away from King Ahab. Go to a river far away. I will keep you safe there."

Did Elijah obey God? Yes, he did. He went to the river. He lived at the river. But he had no food. What will Elijah eat?

Elijah sat down by the river. There was no rain.

There was no food. "What will I do?" Elijah said. "I will trust God."

Then Elijah looked up. What did he see? A bird! A bird came to the river. What did the bird have in its beak? Bread! The bird gave the bread to Elijah.

Elijah picked up the bread. He ate it. He said, "Why did the bird bring me bread?" Then he said, "God sent the bird! I was very hungry, but God sent a bird to feed me."

Then Elijah looked up again. He saw a new bird. This bird had meat in its beak. It gave the meat to Elijah.

"Now I have meat to eat!" cried Elijah. "God sent a bird to give me meat! Did God forget me? No, He did not forget me! He sent birds to bring me food. I will praise God. He remembers me. He will not let me die. He will keep me safe in the famine."

The ravens brought him bread and meat in the morning, and bread and meat in the evening; and he drank from the brook.

(1 Kings 17:6)

Faith Lessons

Ahab trusted in dead idols — Ahab served idols. He trusted his bad idols. But could his idols give him food? Could they send rain? No! His idols were dead. They could not help him.

Elijah obeyed God — God told Elijah to speak to King Ahab. King Ahab did not like what Elijah said. But Elijah still spoke to the king. He told him the word of God. He was not afraid to speak the truth to the king. We must not be afraid to speak the truth.

God cared for Elijah — God sent a famine on the land of Israel. There was no rain. There was no food. Elijah was hungry. He had no food. But God fed him. God did not forget Elijah. He is a very good God.

God rules all things — God made the world, and He rules the world. He rules all things, even birds. God told the birds to bring Elijah food. Did the birds obey? Yes! God is a mighty God. He rules over all.

Vocabulary

Ahab	message	bread
idols	famine	dead
judge	animals	
Elijah	hungry	

CHAPTER 28

Elijah and the Prophets of Baal

Three long years passed. No rain fell on the land of Israel. The people had no food. Will they pray to God? Will they obey God now? God said to Elijah, "Go to King Ahab. Go speak to him."

Elijah went to King Ahab. When Ahab saw Elijah, he was angry. He said, "You stopped the rain! You bring **trouble** on Israel!"

But Elijah said, "I do not bring **trouble** on Israel. You do! You are a wicked man. Your sin brings **trouble** on Israel! God will judge the land for your sin. He will judge the land for the sins of the people."

Then Elijah said, "You do not follow God. You do not follow His commands. You worship false gods. Now call all the prophets of your false gods. Call them all. Let them come here. Then call all the people of Israel."

So King Ahab called all his prophets. His prophets served wicked idols. They served a god named Baal. Now they all came to Elijah. All the people of Israel came to Elijah, too.

Elijah said to the people, "How long will you wait? How long will you worship false gods? If Baal is god, worship him! But if the Lord is God, worship Him!"

Elijah looked at all the people. He looked at the bad prophets. But no one said anything.

Then Elijah said, "I will make an altar. You prophets of Baal, make an altar, too. Kill a bull and put it on the altar. Then pray to your god. Will he send **fire** on your **altar**? Pray to him and ask him to! Then we will see if he is a god."

The prophets of **Baal** made an **altar**. Then they prayed to their god. Did their god hear them? Did he send **fire**? No. He could not hear them. He was a dead god. He was not a real god.

Then Elijah said, "Come here and see." He made an **altar**. He killed a **bull** and put it on the **altar**.

Then he prayed and said, "Lord God, You are the God of Abraham. You are the God of Isaac. You are the God of Jacob. Let the people see that You are the true God of Israel. You are the **only** true God. All other gods are **false**."

Elijah prayed. Then God sent **fire**. It fell on the **altar**. The **fire** came down and burnt up the **bull**.

The people saw this. They were very afraid. They shouted, "The Lord is God! The Lord is God!"

Will the people obey God now?

Now when all the people saw it, they fell on their
faces; and they said, "The LORD, He is God! The
LORD, He is God!"

(1 Kings 18:39)

Faith Lessons

The people forgot God — The people forgot what God did for them. They forgot what God did for Abraham. They forgot what God did for Isaac. They forgot their God. This is sin. We must not forget. We must remember what God did.

God had mercy — The people sinned. They served bad idols. God said, "I will punish them for their sin. I will send a famine." But God had mercy on them, too. He sent Elijah to speak His word to the people. God is a God of mercy.

God made the world. He rules all things — The false idols could not make **fire**. But God could make **fire**. He could send fire on the **altar**. He made all things. He rules all things. He is strong. He is mighty. He is the only true God.

Vocabulary

trouble	Baal	fire
command	anything	only
worship	altar	
false	bull	

CHAPTER 29

God Throws Israel Out of the Good Land

God sent Elijah to speak to the Israelites. Elijah told the people what God said. But did the people obey? No, they did not obey. The people were still wicked. They still sinned. They still served bad gods.

Bad kings ruled in Israel. The kings did wicked things. They did not fear God. They did not trust God. They were not sorry for their sins.

God saw the Israelites. They were wicked. What will God do? Will He **destroy** them?

God said, "I will send prophets. The prophets will tell the people who I am. I am a holy God. I hate sin. The prophets will tell the people to worship Me. They will tell them to stop sinning."

God sent prophets. The prophets spoke the word of God. But the Israelites were not listening. They did not stop serving their bad idols.

Then God said, "I am holy. I hate sin. The people are sinning, and they will not stop. They are very wicked. They are worse than the wicked people around them. They are making people sin with their idols. Now I will judge them for this sin. I will destroy this people. I will destroy the Israelites."

God said, "I gave the Israelites a good land. But they are wicked. Now I will wipe them out of the land. Just like you wipe food off a dish, so I will wipe them off the land. I will make them weak. I will let their enemies beat them. Their enemies will make them slaves. They will take them away to a bad land."

God said, "I will do this to My people. They are wicked. I will punish them for their sin."

God spoke to the people. But what did the people

do? Did they **repent**? No, they did not.

Then God sent strong enemies to Israel. The enemies killed the Israelites. They took the people. They made them slaves. They took them out of the land.

Now God sees His land. It is the land He gave to Abraham. It is the land He gave to Isaac and Jacob. The land has no people in it. God wiped the people off the land. He punished the Israelites for their sin. Now they cannot live in the land.

But God made a covenant with Abraham. He made a covenant with David. Do you remember the covenant? Will God forget His covenant? Will He forget His promise? No, He will not forget.

But what will God do? He has a plan. We must wait to see what His plan is.

> *"So I will forsake [them] . . . because*
> *they have done evil in My sight."*
> *(2 Kings 21:14-15)*

Faith Lessons

The Israelites sinned — The Israelites did not stop sinning. They loved their sin. They liked their wicked gods. They did not **repent**, so God punished them. We must not be like the Israelites. We must not love sin. We must **repent** and pray to God.

God is holy — God is holy. He hates sin. Sin is wicked, so God must punish for sin. He will punish all the world for sin. One day He will come to judge the world.

God will keep His promise — God punished the Israelites for their sin. But He did not forget His covenant. He is a good God. He will keep His promise.

God will send a Seed — How can God keep His promise if His people sin? He will send a Seed to save His people from their sin. He will send Jesus Christ. Jesus will save His people from sin.

Vocabulary

destroy	listening	making
holy	serving	repent
sinning	worse	

CHAPTER 30

God Will Send a Savior

God's people sinned. They did wicked things. They **didn't** obey God.

God said, "I will judge My people. They **don't** listen to Me. I will punish them for their sin. I will wipe them off the land."

Now the people **aren't** in the land. Now they are very sad.

God sees the people. Did He punish them? Yes, He did. But He will have mercy, too. Did He forget His promise? No, He **didn't**. Has He left His people? No,

He **hasn't**. He is still their God.

God spoke to His people. He said, "You sinned. You **didn't** keep My name holy. You **didn't** obey My law. You did very wicked things. I punished you for your sin."

Then God said, "Now I will do a new thing. I will do this to show that I am God. I will do this so that you will honor My name. I will save you from your enemies. I will bring you back to the land I gave to Abraham."

But will the people keep sinning if God brings them back? Yes, they will. God sees this. But He has a plan.

God said, "You can't stop sinning. But I will make you new. I will take out your bad heart. I will put in a new heart. I will make you honor Me. I will make you love Me. Can you love Me? No, you can't. You are wicked. But I will give you a new heart. Then you will love Me."

How can God do this? He will send a Savior. The Savior will save His people from sin. The Savior will make His people love and obey Him. Who is this Savior? Can you tell?

But God **didn't** stop there. He said, "I will send a **Savior**. But My **Savior** will not come just to Israel. He will be a **Savior** to people all over the world. He will call people from all lands to come to Him. He will save them from their sin. He will make them all one people. They will be His people. And He will be their God."

God said, "This is My promise. I will send a **Savior**. He will call people from all lands. He will be a King, and He will have a kingdom. His kingdom will be grand. He will rule forever. His kingdom will not end. It will last forever. This is My promise."

"I will give you a new heart and put a new spirit within you; I will take the heart of stone out of your flesh and give you a heart of flesh."
(Ezekiel 36:26)

Faith Lessons

People can't stop sinning — All people sin. You sin. I sin. We **can't** stop sinning. But God sent a **Savior** to save us from sin. The **Savior** is Jesus.

God will change His people — God will have mercy on His people. He will give them a new **heart**. Now His people will love Him. Now they will worship Him. Now they will follow His law. Now they will be a new people. They will be the people of God.

God will save people from all lands — God will bless all people in all lands. His **Savior** will call people from all lands to come to Him. He will have mercy and will save them. Praise God for His mercy! Praise God for His wisdom! Praise God for His love! He is a very good God! We must praise Him.

Vocabulary

didn't	hasn't	heart
don't	honor	savior
aren't	can't	

CHAPTER 31

The Savior Comes

God's people sinned. They did very bad things. God punished them for their sins. But He still kept His promise to David. He said, "I will send My King. This King will rule forever. He will save His people from their sins."

God said, "I will bring My people back to the land I gave them." He brought some people back. The people lived in the land. Will they trust God now? Will they obey Him?

One day God sent an angel. The angel came to a

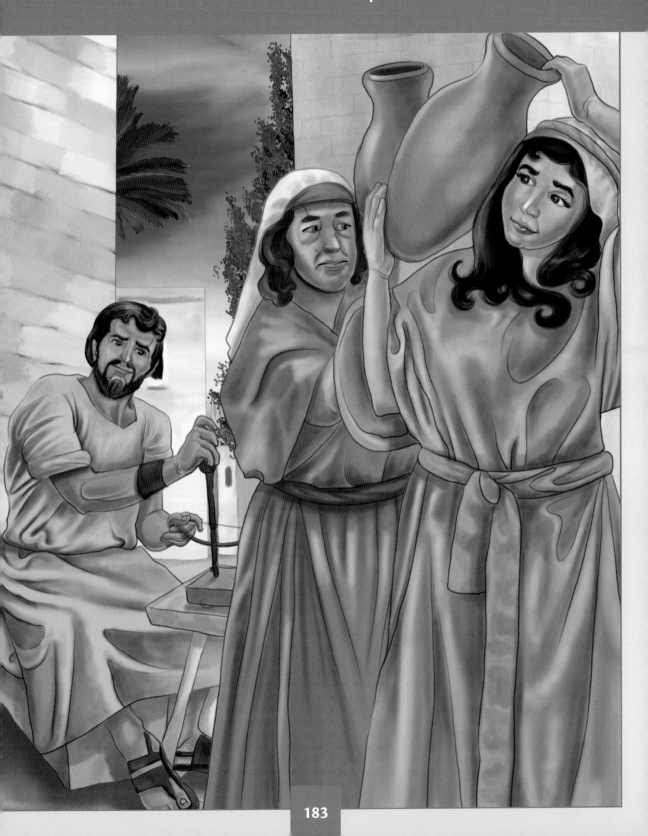

woman. She was from the seed of David. He told the woman, "You will have a son. He will be the Son of God. You will call His name Jesus. He will be a Savior. He will save His people from their sins."

Now God will keep His promise! This is His plan! He will send His own Son to save His people from sin. This is a good plan! God is a good God! He is a wise God! Let us praise Him!

The woman had a baby. She named Him Jesus.

Soon Jesus grew up. He grew into a Man. Is He a Man? Yes, He is a Man. But He is God, too. He is God and Man. He is called **Im-man-u-el**. **Immanuel** means "God with us."

Jesus came to a river. A man was at the river. The man was John. John was **preaching** to the people. He told them to stop sinning. He told them to be sorry for sin. He told them to **believe** in God. Will the people **believe**?

John was **baptizing** the people. Jesus said to John, "Please **baptize** Me." Did John obey? Yes, he did.

John baptized Jesus. The people saw this. Then they saw a new thing. The **Holy Spirit** came to Jesus. Then the people heard a **voice** come from **heaven**. The **voice** was God. God said, "This is My **beloved** Son. I am pleased with Him."

Jesus is the Son of God. God wanted the people to see this. He spoke from **heaven**, and the people heard.

God made the world. He made all things in the world. He made all things good. But Adam and Eve sinned. What did God do? He made a promise. He promised to send a Seed. Now the Seed has come. The Seed is Jesus Christ. He is the Son of God. He will save His people from sin!

And suddenly a voice came from heaven, saying, "This is My beloved Son, in whom I am well pleased." (Matthew 3:17)

Faith Lessons

God kept His promise — A long, long time ago, God made a promise to Adam and Eve. Did God forget His promise? No, He didn't. He remembered His promise and sent His Son. His Son will save His people from sin. Praise God for His Son! Thank Him for sending Jesus!

The people can't stop sinning — John was preaching to the people. He told them to stop sinning. Can the people stop sinning? No, they can't. John will send them to Jesus. Can Jesus save the people from their sin? Yes, He can.

Jesus is the Son of God — God spoke from heaven. He let all the people hear. He wanted all the people to see that Jesus was God. He wants us to see this, too. Will you believe God? Will you believe Jesus?

Vocabulary

Immanuel	baptize	voice
preaching	baptizing	heaven
believe	Holy Spirit	beloved

CHAPTER 32

The Devil Tempts Jesus

Jesus is the Son of God. He came to save His people from sin. He is God. He is a good God.

But the devil did not want Jesus to save His people. He wanted to stop Jesus. Can the devil stop Him?

The Holy Spirit led Jesus into the desert. Now Jesus had no food to eat. He stayed in the desert 40 days. He was **hungry**. Then the devil came to Him.

The devil said, "I will **tempt** Jesus. I will make Him sin. Then He will not be good. Then He can't save His people from sin."

The devil said to Jesus, "You are **hungry**. You have no food. But here are rocks. If You are God, You can turn a rock into food. Speak to this rock. Make it turn into **bread**."

Did Jesus obey the devil? No, He didn't. He said, "The Word of God says, 'Man must not live by **bread alone**. Man will live by the Word of God.'" People need God's Word more than they need food. Jesus will obey God's Word. He will not obey the devil.

Then the devil took Jesus to the **temple**. He took Him up to the top of the **temple**. Then he said, "If You are the Son of God, jump off the top of the **temple**! God will keep You safe. He will send His angels to keep You safe."

Did Jesus obey the devil? No! It would be sin to jump off the **temple**. It would be sin to **tempt** God. We must not do **silly** things that might hurt us.

Jesus said, "God's Word says, 'Do not tempt God.' I will not jump off the temple. I will not tempt God."

Then the devil said, "I will tempt Jesus one more time." He took Jesus to the top of a big mountain. He showed Him all the kingdoms of the world. He said, "All the kingdoms are mine. But I will give them to You if You will worship me."

Will Jesus listen to the devil? No, He will not!

Jesus said, "Get away from Me! I will not worship you! The Word of God tells us to worship God **alone**. We must not worship any other thing."

Could the devil make Jesus sin? No, he could not. Jesus is God. He will not sin.

The devil is not strong. He is not strong like God.

Then the devil left Jesus. He ran away. He was sad. He could not make Jesus sin.

*Then Jesus said to him, "Away with you, Satan! For it is written, 'You shall worship the L*ORD *your God, and Him only you shall serve.'"*

(Matthew 4:10)

Faith Lessons

Jesus is God — Jesus is God. He can't sin. We sin. We listen to the devil. But Jesus will not sin. He will not obey the devil. He is God.

Jesus was tempted, but He didn't sin — Did the devil **tempt** Jesus? Yes, he did. Jesus got **hungry** just like we get **hungry**. Then the devil **tempted** Him just like he **tempts** us. But Jesus didn't sin.

The devil is not strong like God — The devil wants to be strong. He wants to fight God. But he can't win. He is not strong like God. He is weak. God will not let him win.

God's word is a sword — The devil is a wicked enemy. How did Jesus fight him? He took God's word for His **sword**. The Bible is **powerful**. It is our **sword**, too. It will teach us what God is like. And it will teach us how to fight sin, too.

Vocabulary

hungry	alone	sword
tempt	temple	powerful
tempted	silly	
bread	mountain	

CHAPTER 33

Jesus Heals a Sick Man

A man had a problem. He was sick. He was very sick. And he **couldn't** get well. He had a bad **sickness**. The **doctors couldn't** help the man. They **couldn't** fix his **sickness**. No one could help him. He would die from his **sickness**. He would **never** get well.

The man was very sad. He **couldn't** live with other people. He might get the other people sick. He had to live alone. His **body** hurt. He did not like it to hurt. But he **couldn't** stop it. He **couldn't** get well. He would die from his sickness.

But then the man heard a person. The person said, "Jesus is here. Jesus is healing people."

The man said, "Who is Jesus? Can He heal people? Can He make sick people well? Who is He?"

A person said, "He is the Son of God."

Will the man go to Jesus? Could Jesus help him? Could Jesus heal him? Could Jesus stop his sickness?

The man said, "I am sick. I have a bad sickness. It will kill me. Can Jesus help? If He is the Son of God, He can help. He can heal my sickness. He can make my body well. He can make it clean."

Then the man said, "If Jesus is the Son of God, He is the Lord. He can heal me. But will He heal me? Will He want to heal me? Is He a good Lord?"

The man said, "I will go to Jesus. I will see if He is a good Lord. I will ask Him to heal me." He ran to find Jesus. Will he find Him? Yes, he will.

The man did find Jesus. He fell down on the ground in front of Jesus. Then he said, "Lord, if You want to, You can heal me. If You are willing, You can make me well."

Is Jesus willing? Will He want to heal the man? Yes!

Jesus saw the man. He saw his bad **sickness**. Then He put His hand on the man. He said, "I am willing. I want to heal you. Now you will be clean. Now you will not be sick."

Jesus healed the man. Now the man is very happy! He is healed! He **isn't** sick!

God is a good God! Jesus is a good Lord! Let us praise Him! He will heal a sick man! He will make him well!

Then He put out His hand and touched him, saying,
"I am willing; be cleansed."
(Luke 5:13)

Faith Lessons

Jesus is God — The sick man said, "A **doctor** can't heal me. But God can heal me." Jesus healed the man. Jesus is God.

We are like the sick man — The sick man **couldn't** get well. He **couldn't** fix his **sickness**. We are like the sick man. We are sick with sin. We can't fix this **sickness**. But Jesus can fix it. He is God, and He can save us from sin. He can save us just like He saved the man from **sickness**.

Jesus rules the world — Jesus made the world. He rules the world. He rules all things. All things must obey Him. Even **sickness** must obey Him. Jesus is God.

Vocabulary

couldn't	doctor	healing
isn't	never	
sickness	body	

CHAPTER 34

The Last Supper

God has a plan. When Adam sinned, God said, "I will send a Seed. He will crush the devil. The Seed will save Adam from sin. He will save all His people from sin."

What is God's plan? God's plan is Jesus. Jesus is the Seed. God promised to send a Seed. Now the Seed is here.

Jesus is God. Then He became Man. Why did He become Man? He said, "I will save My people from sin. I will come to earth. I will die for My people. I will pay for their sins. I will save them from their sins."

Jesus came to earth. He preached to the people. Did He teach? Yes, He did. He called 12 men. The 12 men were His disciples. The disciples heard Jesus teach. They followed Him.

Jesus said, "I came to earth. I came to save My people. I came to die for them. I want My disciples to see this. I will teach them that I came to die."

Jesus called His 12 disciples. They went into a room. Then they had supper. Jesus took the bread. He broke the bread and gave it to His disciples. Then He said, "This is My body. I will give My body for you."

Then Jesus took a cup of wine. He gave the wine to His disciples. He said, "Drink this. This is My blood. I will give My blood for you."

Then Jesus said, "Do this to remember Me."

The disciples ate the bread. They drank the wine. Did they under-stand? Did they understand that

Jesus would die for them?

Jesus looked at His **disciples**. His **disciples** did not **understand**. They didn't **know** what He would do. They said, "We don't **know** what His words mean."

The **disciples** didn't **understand**. They were weak. They were **sinful**. But Jesus loved them. He said, "My **disciples** are weak. They don't **understand** Me. But I still love them. I will love them to the end. I will die for them. I have come to save them from their sin."

And He took bread, gave thanks and broke it, and gave it to them, saying, "This is My body which is given for you."

(Luke 22:19)

Faith Lessons

God has a plan — God made a promise when Adam sinned. Now God will keep His promise. Jesus will save His people from sin. This is a good plan! God is a good God! Let us praise Him!

Jesus loves His disciples — Jesus came to earth. He called people. He said, "Follow Me." He loves His disciples. He will give them a new heart so they can love Him, too. The disciples sin. But Jesus still loves them. He will love them forever.

Jesus came to die — Jesus chose a people. But His people sin. All people sin. How can God fix this? He will come to die for His people. He will pay for their sin. He is a God of mercy. We must thank Him for His mercy!

Vocabulary

became	disciple	sinful
become	understand	heart
earth	know	

CHAPTER 35

The Night in the Garden

God made all things. He made all things good. God looked at the world He made. He said, "It is very good."

But then Adam and Eve sinned. They did not obey God. This is sin. They broke God's law. This is sin, too. Now God looks at the world He made. "I see sin," He said. "I hate sin. I am **holy**. But sin is wicked. I must **judge** Adam. I must punish him for his sin. If he sins, he must die."

God is a **holy** God. Sin can't live with Him. He

must punish sin. If you sin, you must die. You can't live with God. God will send you to hell. This is how wicked sin is.

Did God **judge** Adam? Did He kill Adam for his sin? No, He didn't. God said, "I will have mercy. I will send a Seed. I will send Jesus. He will die for Adam. He will die for Adam's sin. Then Adam can live with Me. Then I can **forgive** Adam for his sin."

Jesus came to die for sin. Did Jesus sin? No! He is **perfect**. He is God. But He said, "I will become Man. I will come to earth to die for sin. Then My people can live with Me." This is very good news! We call this the **Gospel**.

Now it was time for Jesus to die. He called His disciples. They went to a garden. It was night. The disciples were **tired**. Jesus said, "Wait here and stay **awake**. I will go pray. Then I will come back."

Jesus went to be alone. He prayed to God. This was

a hard night. Jesus would die for sin. But this was hard work. God is a **perfect** God. He is **holy**. That means He must be angry at people for sin. Jesus said, "I will take God's anger. I will take the **punishment** for sin."

This was very hard. So Jesus prayed. Then He came back to His disciples. Were they **awake**? No, they were sleeping!

Jesus asked, "Can't you stay **awake** with Me for a little time?"

The disciples are weak. They are sinful. Jesus sees this. He says, "The time is here. Now I will die for them. They are weak. They are full of sin. But I will love them to the end."

Then He said to them,
"My soul is exceedingly sorrowful, even to death.
Stay here and watch with Me."
(Matthew 26:38)

Faith Lessons

It is hard to pay for sin — You sin and I sin. We do bad things. We think it's okay to sin. But it isn't okay. Sin is very wicked. God must punish sin. He will judge us. He will send people to hell for their sin. It is very hard to pay for sin.

Jesus paid for sin — Jesus said, "I will die for sin. I will take the punishment for My people." We must trust in Jesus. He will pay for His people's sin.

Jesus loves His people — The disciples sin. They can't even stay awake for Jesus! But Jesus is full of mercy. He will not leave His disciples. He will love them to the end.

God is very good — God is holy. He is perfect. He must punish sin. So God said, "I will send a Seed to save My people from sin." God is full of mercy. He is very good! Praise Him!

Vocabulary

holy	perfect	awake
judge	gospel	punishment
forgive	tired	

CHAPTER 36

Jesus Dies on the Cross

Jesus and His disciples are in a garden. Jesus is praying to God. It is night. But **someone else** is in the garden. Who is it? It is a big **crowd**.

The **crowd** of men come up to Jesus. The **crowd** has swords. They are looking for Jesus. They want to kill Him.

Jesus said, "Who are you looking for?"

"We are looking for Jesus," they said.

"I am He," Jesus told them.

Then the men were afraid. They fell back and fell

down to the ground. They were afraid of Jesus. But they wanted to kill Him, too.

Jesus knows the men want to kill Him. Will He fight? No, He **won't** fight. He will go with the men. He will die for His people.

The men took Jesus. They tied Him up and took Him away. His disciples saw this. They were afraid. Will they fight for Jesus? No, they **won't**. They ran away to hide.

The men took Jesus to the rulers. The rulers said, "Jesus must die!" Did Jesus do **anything** bad? No, He didn't! He shouldn't die! But the rulers were wicked. They wanted to kill Jesus.

The rulers sent Jesus to **Pilate**. **Pilate** was a strong ruler. He didn't want to kill Jesus. He said, "Jesus didn't do **anything** bad. He shouldn't die." But the **crowd** said, "Kill Him!"

Pilate was afraid of the **crowd**. He didn't want the

crowd to get mad at him, so he said, "Take Jesus and kill Him."

The **soldiers** took Jesus. They beat Him. Then they put Him on a cross and killed Him.

It was day when the **soldiers** put Jesus on the cross. But the sun stopped shining. The sky became dark like night. The people saw this. They were afraid.

When Jesus died, the ground shook. The rocks broke. The people saw this, too. The **soldiers** saw it and were afraid. One soldier said, "This Man was the Son of God!"

The disciples of Jesus were very sad. Now Jesus had died. Wicked men had killed Him.

A **friend** of Jesus came. He took the body of Jesus and put it in a **tomb**. Then the **soldiers** rolled a big stone up to the door of the **tomb**.

The disciples saw the **tomb**. They saw the big stone. Then they went away. They were very sad.

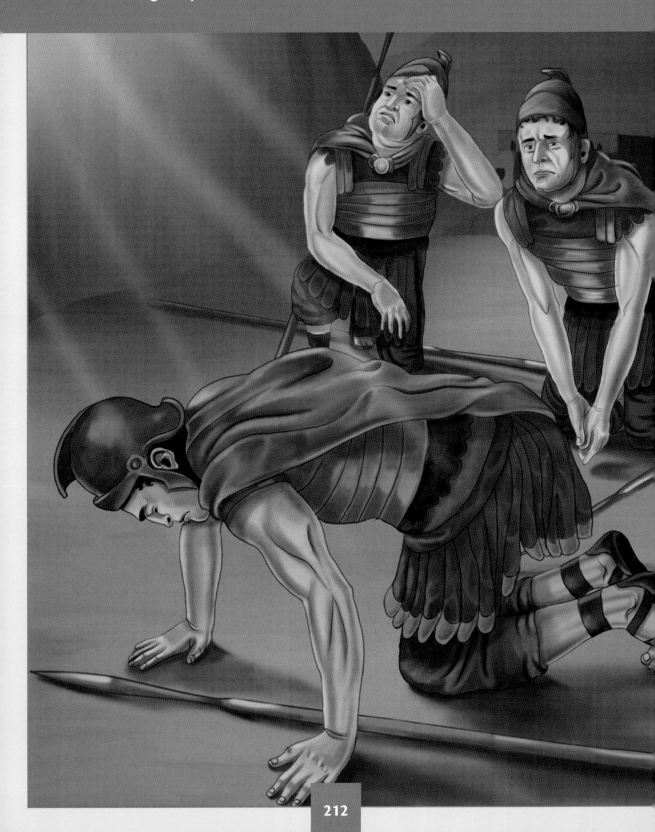

They went away and cried. They didn't want Jesus to die.

But God had a plan. This was part of His plan. Do you remember what His plan was?

They feared greatly, saying,
"Truly this was the Son of God!"
(Matthew 27:54)

Faith Lessons

Jesus didn't fight — The crowd was afraid of Jesus. Jesus is God. He made the crowd. He could kill the crowd. But He didn't. He went with the wicked men. He let them kill Him. This was His plan. It is a good plan. He is a very good God!

Pilate was afraid, so he sinned — Pilate said, "Jesus shouldn't die." But he was afraid of the crowd. He didn't want the crowd to get mad at him, so he killed Jesus. We must not be like Pilate. We must not be afraid of people. We must do what is right even when people get mad. We must fear God. We must not fear people.

Jesus died for His people — Jesus loves His people. He died for them. Why did He die? He died to save them from sin. Let us thank Him for His love! Let us praise Him for what He did!

Vocabulary

someone	won't	soldiers
else	anything	friend
crowd	Pilate	tomb

CHAPTER 37

Jesus Rises from the Dead

Jesus was **dead**. His body was in the tomb. A big stone blocked the front of the tomb. No one could get in. No one could get out. Soldiers stood by the tomb to **guard** it.

Jesus is perfect. He is God. He didn't sin. But He still died. Why? Why did He die? Do you remember?

Jesus died for sin. He said, "I will become Man. I will come to earth to die for sin. Then My people can live with Me." This is very good news!

But Jesus is God. He didn't stay **dead**. On the third

day after He died, He came back to life.

On **Sunday** morning, an **angel** came down. The ground shook. The soldiers at the tomb were afraid. They fell to the ground like they were **dead**. Then the

angel rolled away the stone by the tomb. Jesus wasn't **dead anymore**. Now He is alive!

Some women came to the tomb. They felt the ground shake. Then they saw the **angel**. They were very afraid.

But the **angel** said, "Don't be afraid. Come and see. The Lord is not here. He has **risen**. He is alive!"

The women came and looked. The tomb was **empty**! They ran to tell the disciples. The disciples didn't **believe** them. "We know Jesus is **dead**!" they said. Then they ran to the tomb, too. It was **empty**!

"Is Jesus alive?" the disciples asked. They didn't know.

Then Jesus came to them. He showed them that He was alive. Now the disciples **believe**. Now they will fall down and worship Him. He is alive! He is the Son of God!

But the angel answered and said to the women, "Do not be afraid, for I know that you seek Jesus who was crucified. He is not here; for He is risen, as He said."

(Matthew 28:5-6)

Faith Lessons

Jesus rose from the dead — Jesus died. But He didn't stay dead. On the third day, He came out of the tomb. He is alive! One day we will die. All people will die. But God will raise us from the dead, too.

Jesus is Lord — Jesus is the Lord of all the world. One day He will judge the world. One day all people will rise from the dead. Then Jesus will judge them. Some will go to hell for their sin. But Jesus will save His people. He died for them. They will not go to hell. They will live with Him forever.

The disciples believed — The disciples were afraid. They didn't understand. But then Jesus came to them. Then they believed. We must believe Jesus, too. He is God. He came to save His people from sin. We must be sorry for sin and believe in Him just like His disciples.

Jesus rose from the dead on Sunday — On Sunday morning, Jesus left the tomb. Sunday is called the Lord's Day. Why? This is the day He rose from the dead. This is the day we meet to worship Him. All over the world, people meet on **Sunday** to worship the Lord who rose from the **dead**!

Vocabulary

dead	angel	empty
guard	anymore	believe
Sunday	risen	

CHAPTER 38

Jesus Rises Up to Heaven

Jesus was alive! His disciples were filled with **joy**. They were very glad to have Jesus back with them. But they still didn't understand all that Jesus did.

Jesus saw that His disciples didn't understand. He said, "I will teach you what these things mean. Do you remember what the **Scripture** says? It speaks of Me. Do you remember what **happened** long, long ago? Adam and Eve sinned. Then what did God do? He promised to send a Seed. The Seed would crush the devil. The Seed would save His people from sin."

Jesus said, "I am the Seed. I crushed the devil. I beat him. Now he can't hurt you anymore. Now he can't make you his slave. I have **rescued** you. You are My people, and I have saved you. I have saved you from the devil."

Jesus told them, "I have saved you from sin, too. You all sin. You can't stop sinning. But I have saved you from sin. Now you can fight sin. I will give you **strength**. I will make you strong. I will send the Holy Spirit. He will teach you of Me. He will teach you to fight sin. And He will make you strong to preach My word."

Then Jesus said, "God made a promise to David. Do you remember? He promised to send a King who would rule forever. I am that King. I am the Son of David. I will rule forever. I have all **power**. I am God. I rule all things. And I will rule forever. My kingdom

will never end."

One day Jesus and His disciples went to a mountain. Jesus spoke to them on the mountain. He said, "God the Father has put all power in My hands. I have all **power** in heaven and on earth. Now I will send you. Go and make disciples of all **nations**. Teach all people the things I **commanded** you. And remember that I am **always** with you."

Jesus blessed His disciples. Then He went up into heaven. The disciples saw Him go up into the sky. Then an angel came to them. He said, "Men, why do you look up at the sky? Jesus went up into heaven. One day He will come back just like you saw Him go."

The disciples believed. They praised God and feared Him.

*And Jesus came and spoke to them, saying, . . . "I am with you **always**, even to the end of the age." Amen.*
(Matthew 28:18, 20)

Faith Lessons

Jesus crushed the devil — The devil couldn't win. Jesus crushed him. The devil has no power to fight God. No bad thing can fight God. God will always win. We don't need to be afraid of bad things or bad people. We must trust God. He will win the fight.

All the Bible speaks of Jesus — From the first part to the very last, all the Bible tells us of Jesus. We must read it all. We must learn from it all. It is the Word of God. It will tell us of the good and loving God we serve.

Jesus has all power — Jesus is God. He has all power. He rules all the world. His kingdom will last forever.

Jesus sent His people to teach all nations — Jesus wants His people to tell all people of Him. He sent His disciples to every nation. All the world must hear the good news of Jesus.

Vocabulary

joy	strength	commanded
Scripture	power	always
happened	father	
rescued	nation	

CHAPTER 39

God Sends the Holy Spirit

One day the disciples of Jesus got **together** in a room. It was a big room with over 100 people in it!

Why did the people get **together**? They came to pray. Jesus was in heaven. But He made a promise to His people. Do you remember His promise? He said He would send the Holy Spirit to them.

That day, the men and women were gathered in a room. They were praying. **Suddenly**, they heard a sound. The sound came from heaven. It sounded like a strong wind. And it filled the house!

The people looked around. They saw **fire**! It looked like flames of **fire** over each person. Then the people were filled with the Holy Spirit. They began to speak. They began to tell people **about** Jesus. They began to preach the Bible.

People from all over the world were near the house. They heard God's people preach. But they got a big **surprise**. The disciples spoke in **many languages**.

"How do they know my **language**?" the people asked. Some people were from Egypt. Some were from Rome. They came from all over the world. But they heard the men speak their own **language**. They were **amazed**.

Then Peter said, "God promised to send His Holy Spirit. This is why we speak your **language**. He sent us to tell you **about** Jesus. You killed Jesus. But God

raised Him from the dead. Now He will rule forever. He is the king God promised to David. His kingdom is here. And He will rule forever."

The people heard Peter. They were afraid. They said, "What should we do?"

Peter said, "**Repent** of your sins. Be sorry for your sins. Then come and be baptized. God will give you the Holy Spirit. Jesus died for sins. He tells you to come and **repent**. He made this promise to you. He made it to your children. He made it to all people who are near and who are far away. He made this promise to as **many** as He will call."

Then the people believed Jesus. They were sorry for their sins. Did they **repent**? Yes, they did. They were glad to hear Peter speak. They were glad to hear the good news he told them. They came to be baptized. Three thousand people came!

The men didn't stop preaching. They told people

about God. They told people about sin. Then they
told them about what Jesus did. God gave them
wisdom. He gave them power to speak. They were
bold and brave. And God kept adding more and more
people to His church.

Then Peter said to them, "Repent, and let every one
of you be baptized in the name of Jesus Christ."

(Acts 2:38)

Faith Lessons

God kept His promise — Jesus said that He would send His Holy Spirit. Did He keep His promise? Yes, He did! He always keeps His promises! We can trust Him!

The Holy Spirit made God's people brave — The disciples were afraid. But the Holy Spirit came to them and made them brave. Then they spoke to the people about God. They were not afraid to preach anymore. Now they were bold.

Jesus sent His people to teach and preach — Jesus said, "Go and make disciples of all nations. Teach all people the things I commanded you." He wants us to tell all nations about Him. Let us obey Him!

Vocabulary

together	surprise	repent
suddenly	many	bold
fire	language	
about	amazed	

CHAPTER 40

A Prison Guard Believes

Paul and Silas were in prison. It was a dark prison. It was a cold prison. They were hungry. They were hurt. They were chained down.

Why were Paul and Silas in prison? Why were they hurt? They had preached to the people. They told them about Jesus. They preached in a city called Philippi. The people heard them preach. They heard about Jesus. But some people got angry. They wanted Paul and Silas to stop preaching.

What did the angry people do? They took Paul and Silas. They beat them. Then they put them in prison. What will happen now?

Were Paul and Silas sad? Were they angry at the bad men? No. What did they do? They prayed. Then they praised God. "Let us sing to God," they said. So they sang in the cold, dark prison.

Suddenly, the earth shook. It was an earthquake! The prison shook. All the chains broke. The prison doors stood open. Now Paul and Silas were free!

What did Paul and Silas do? Did they run away? Did they leave the prison? No, not yet.

The guard at the prison came. He saw the broken chains. He saw the open doors. He said, "The prisoners will escape! The rulers will kill me! I will kill myself." The man took a sword. He said, "I will kill myself with my sword."

But Paul said, "Don't kill yourself! We didn't

escape! We are all still here!"

The man came to Paul. He was afraid. He fell down in front of Paul. "How can I be saved?" he asked.

Paul said, "Believe in Jesus Christ. Then you and your family will be saved."

The man believed. He took Paul and Silas out of the prison. He took them to his house. Then Paul spoke the Word of God to the man. He spoke to his family. The man and his family believed God's Word. They were very glad to hear it!

Then the man gave Paul and Silas food to eat. He took care of them.

Paul and Silas were very happy. Why were they happy? They were glad that the man believed God. They were glad that his family believed God. God sent Paul and Silas to preach. Now God had saved the man and his family. Paul and Silas praised God. He is a very good God!

So they said, "Believe on the Lord Jesus Christ, and you will be saved, you and your household." Then they spoke the word of the Lord to him and to all who were in his house.

(Acts 16:31-32)

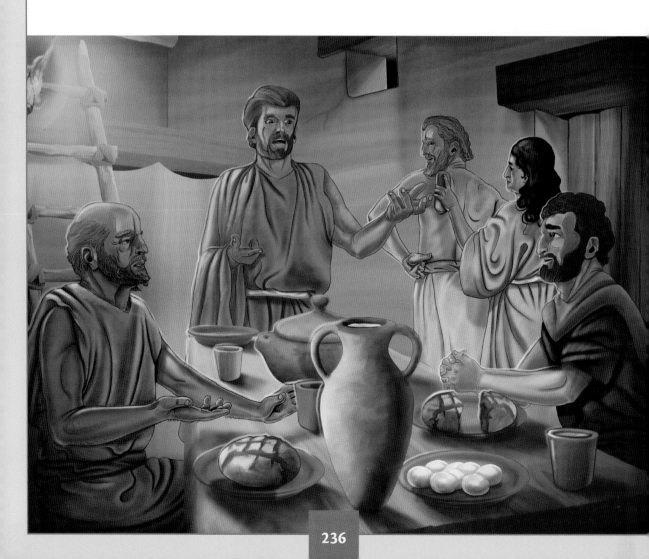

Faith Lessons

Paul and Silas did not get angry in prison — Bad men hurt Paul and Silas. They put them in prison. But Paul and Silas did not get angry. They prayed to God. They praised God. They said, "God is stronger than bad men. We will trust God."

God had a plan — Paul and Silas did not do anything bad. But they were sent to prison. But God had a plan. He put Paul and Silas in prison. Why? He put them there so that the guard could hear about Jesus. This was a good plan! God is a good God!

God's kingdom is growing — God sends His people to preach. Paul and Silas preached. Then God saved people from sin. He saved the guard and his family. God's kingdom grows. It is growing all over the world!

Vocabulary

Paul	Philippi	myself
Silas	earthquake	yourself
prison	prisoner	